Near Death Experiences

The Ultimate Guide to the Nde and Its Aftereffects

(Verified Paranormal Phenomena From Near-death Experiences)

Andrea Abram

Published By **Zoe Lawson**

Andrea Abram

All Rights Reserved

Near Death Experiences: The Ultimate Guide to the Nde and Its Aftereffects (Verified Paranormal Phenomena From Near-death Experiences)

ISBN 978-1-77485-742-7

No part of this guidebook shall be reproduced in any form without permission in writing from the publisher except in the case of brief quotations embodied in critical articles or reviews.

Legal & Disclaimer

The information contained in this ebook is not designed to replace or take the place of any form of medicine or professional medical advice. The information in this ebook has been provided for educational & entertainment purposes only.

The information contained in this book has been compiled from sources deemed reliable, and it is accurate to the best of the Author's knowledge; however, the Author cannot guarantee its accuracy and validity and cannot be held liable for any errors or omissions. Changes are periodically made to this book. You must consult your doctor or get professional medical advice before using any of the suggested remedies, techniques, or information in this book.

Upon using the information contained in this book, you agree to hold harmless the Author from and against any damages, costs, and expenses, including any legal fees potentially resulting from the application of any of the information provided by this guide. This disclaimer applies to any damages or injury caused by the use and application, whether directly or indirectly, of any advice or information presented, whether for breach of contract, tort, negligence, personal injury, criminal intent, or under any other cause of action.

You agree to accept all risks of using the information presented inside this book. You need to consult a professional medical practitioner in order to ensure you are both able and healthy enough to participate in this program.

TABLE OF CONTENTS

Introduction 1

Chapter 1: What Is The Near Death Experience? 3

Chapter 2: Worldwide Phenomena 17

Chapter 3: Angels And The Role Of Angels 33

Chapter 4: The Real World Examples Of The Near Death Experience 42

Chapter 5: The History Of The Near Death Experience 99

Chapter 6: Psychological Consequences 125

Chapter 7: Near Death Experience Hell Following Suicide Attempt 140

Chapter 8: Near Death Experience And Haunting 162

Conclusion 183

Introduction

The term "near dying experience" is a powerful evocation. While for some , it could just be an indication of the proximity of an accident or tragic event in their lives, for others the significance of a near-death event is often a lot more spiritual.

If you've experienced the near-death experience (or NDE), the experience isn't only one of the most serious health issues or deaths. The process of coming near the end of your life and then returning enough to raise questions about what is beyond this realm of existence, and also what their passing signifies to a larger world. For those who were unfortunate enough to suffer an NDE it can be devastating, life-affirming, frightening and can be a life-changing moment.

The experiences of those affected by near-death experiences may differ greatly. There are usually similarities however, the most intriguing aspects of this phenomenon result from the small differences in the accounts given by those who've stepped towards death only to return to tell their story.

If a person is diagnosed as dead or has been in danger of dying the development of medical technology has definitely increased our capacity to save lives. Additionally it has also blurred the lines between living people and dead, transforming the point where we can be able to define a person as being beyond the realm of existence. For those who've had close-to-death experiences, what details about stories, experiences, and other information are they able to share with the world at large?

Chapter 1: What Is The Near Death Experience?

The first thing we need to do is identify the near-death experience. It can be a challenge because some of the most well-known experiences differing significantly in specifics. There are some commonalities and common experiences that aid in defining the events, and also assist us in understanding the events that people are experiencing.

The most important thing is always the existence of the individual. These are events that we refer to as "near death events" due to their closeness to death. Since there is an end-of-life quality to living, and the capacity to be so close to death and return gives these events a reverence character, particularly in comparison with the more mundane experiences we can experience in our daily lives.

Although it is an unpalatable and taboo issue in some societies, contemplations and ideas about what happens after death are fascinating to many of people. Due to this, people who are able to provide insight and ideas regarding this are usually given platforms to express their views. If we are trying to define the near-death event, our own mortality as human beings will always have a significant role to play.

A lot of people are close to dying frequently. In normal circumstances you could have been involved in an accident in the car or through the steps, or suffer an extended illness or be the victim of a violent crimes. Although these events can lead us to death, they're not exactly what we would consider an experience that is close to death. To understand this specific label and to comprehend this specific phenomenon it is crucial to realize that there is a second component.

In this regard, many people that investigate experiences of NDEs usually observe some aspect of supernatural spiritual, the religious, or simply outright bizarre. There could be a feeling of levitation, an ex-body experience, seeing angels and/or demons. It could also be an overwhelming sense of peace or even a feeling comfortable and warm. These sensations that are abstract distinguishes the experience of near death from just a mere near death. Instead of being an actual medical procedure it is a spiritual experience. Instead of simply transferring from one state of being to another individuals who have returned from the brink often inform us about their experiences, and how they differ from anything else they have experienced prior to.

There is a need to research and understand more about the near-death experience. Because it is difficult to measure and harder to reproduce, studies into the phenomenon are typically shrewd stabs into the darkness. If you are looking for answers regarding the NDE is not likely to offer rational explanations. For certain people it makes the narratives concerning near-death experiences difficult to believe. For others, it's why they are so fascinating.

Avoiding straightforward and simple answers, we're left with ample space for reflection and interpretation. Similar to the way that we can be presented with the facts of a tale and come up with different interpretations the near-death experience gives listeners, participants as well as observers and skeptical people the chance to learn more about what's taking place. As with other experiences that occur in the course of a person's life it is often no certain answers. This is the reason for an enormous amount of curiosity about the NDE and helps to explain the public's fascination into what is very personal and very subjective experience.

How can we best define the near death experience?
The most important thing is that a person is close to dying and , in dying, experiences an experience that is spiritual in nature. It is possible you are judged dead, though this isn't essential and prior to being restored, they are confronted with an experience or

vision that is different from anything they've had before.

Based on these essential aspects are a number of points that could help clarify our understanding of what NDE actually means. Bruce Greyson, a researcher who is the source of a lot of the information we have about NDEs, has described the broad categories of experiences common to many who have near-death experiences.

According to Greyson As suggested by Greyson, there can be the sensation of being out of their body, and is observing the events happening within the immediate area. It could be that someone is watching surgeons perform surgeries on them, or watching first responders removing them from a wrecked car. Visions can come up of distant relatives or those who have passed away such as a grandfather that has passed away, or a sibling that is thousands kilometers away. Greyson is also a description of the regularity that boundaries are easily breached, regardless of whether they are related to time or space. It could be that seconds seem like hours, or the reverse is true. It could be that the moment transports people many thousands of miles, or brings them closer to their loved ones.

Although not every experience is similar and all experiences share the similar characteristics, these traits are often the basis for what is commonly thought of as a near-death experience. When it comes to near-death experiences, that is the thing we usually think of. We will discover in the future they can be completely unique and exciting.

The history of the Near Death Experience
As opposed to many aspects of the spiritual and the unknowable, advancements in the fields of science and medicine are able to recognize and record more near-death experiences, as well as the amount of information available to the public on these experiences. For researchers, this boils related to two major reasons:

* The advances in medical understanding and techniques.

* Our ability to share information more efficiently

As we've become more adept in treating illness and injury caused through accidents, our ability to heal and revive is higher than ever. The advancements in technology have meant that the chances of helping people return from death's edge have increased more than they ever were before.

In addition the wide usage on the web, the 24-hour television news, as well as the constant publication of books means that we have the capability to communicate with one another of NDEs, more than previously in human history.

Because of the work by historians, we are able to find stories of near-death incidents that are recorded over the years. Primarily-sourced accounts and firsthand accounts are difficult to locate because of the huge amount of time gone by, the deficiency of literacy, and also the scarce printing materials that are durable. But, some texts like those in the Bible or the Koran are among the most popular texts of all time, and both provide evidence of NDE.

The first version is more ancient than any of these texts. It is believed that the Greek philosopher Plato provides a description of what he describes as sounding similar to a near death incident in the tenth volume of his renowned Republic.

Plato is a student of the School of Athens painted by Raphael in 1509

The reader discovers Er an army soldier who is laid to rest on an effigy of a funeral and believed as dead. After waking up at the very final minute, Er tells everyone about his journey to the next life. For Plato his story of Er is more than an incident. The elements of the tale were interspersed into the larger philosophical argument in his work. The shining of the truth and the path through the mind as an ethereal entity, and a vision of the light are aspects that we can consider to be identical to the stories of many contemporary authors.

If you are looking for precise information within the Bible There have been numerous disagreements. For instance, a significant majority of people utilize 2 Corinthians 12:2-5 to prove for the biblical concept of an NDE. It could appear as an interpretation that is in line with the requirements of the interpreter who wants to play around with the scripture, but believing that Paul was technically dead prior to entering heaven's kingdom is certainly an NDE.

Although it isn't mentioned in the text however, many choose to believe that this was the result of a near-death experience. If it was a dream or a real-life experience, the desire to investigate and interpret the tale by people across the years can be considered to be evidence of a sense of awareness and necessity to comprehend near-death experiences.

Another problem with the interpretation of Biblical texts is the role and presence in the role of Satan throughout the texts. In the Bible Satan is a deceitful and unreliable person who can alter the minds of those who he meets. If you are looking through the books like Corinthians Skeptics have pointed out the role played by Satan as possibly deceiving. If Satan is able to cover himself up as an angel then the credibility of the near-death incident is questioned.

In some ways it is true that the Bible isn't open about the subject. But, the deeper theological issues that are raised by the Bible and the stories of Jesus could help to gain a better understanding of the beliefs that underlie many of the theories that people have about the NDE phenomenon. Jesus' numerous description of the trip to heaven and soul-related qualities (Luke 10:25-28; Romans 8:39 and other passages) are a great way to expand our knowledge about the stories of our ancestors' regarding these encounters. In gaining a better understanding of their beliefs in theology, we can complete the gaps that lacking sources and primary texts have not been able to fill. Much in the same as Plato's account tells what we know the truth about Greek understandings about the NDE The Bible provides readers with an historical Christian viewpoint on these experiences.

Another fascinating area of historical inquiry is the field of medicine. As previously mentioned the increased capabilities of doctors means there is not just an increased probability of patients recovering however, there is a growing desire to record their experiences. Our oldest medical record of this kind of event is from an French doctor in the middle of the 18th century.

In 1740, Pierre-Jean du Monchaux leaves us his personal memoirs of his time as a physician in the military posted in the northern region of France. He wrote a book called Anecdotes de Medecine, a collection of anecdotes and stories of his experiences in caring for patients. In the description of patients who have an NDE the doctor explains that any NDE is caused by too much blood flowing into the head and the brain being overwhelmed by a sudden surge when the patient regains consciousness.

One present figure studying the near-death incident is a Frenchman. The Dr. Philippe Charlier is not only a physician but also an archaeologist too. He is highly respected in his country of origin as a forensic researcher of historical individuals. As part of his general study, Charlier happened across another ancient description of a man in a book that he bought from an antique store.

In an interview with Live Science, Charlier described his fascination with the history of medicine, as well as in the methods that have developed and changed into what we are today. The time frame he's interested in is the 18th century, which is the period during which the book he found in his store finds were written. Although it isn't a classic book however, it did offer fascinating reading on the story of the near-death incident.

In the book in the book, a famous pharmacist (an an apothecary as they were called in the day) in Paris was sucked into a state of unconsciousness. When he awoke, he talks about seeing an incredible clear and brilliant light that is like heaven to him.

In the early days, lack of understanding or information regarding the near-death incident led to rejection and curiosity. What we now consider as life-changing and profound were at times misinterpreted. According to Charlier states the people of the time were more inclined to believe that the events were caused by the supernatural. In the course of other studies and research He also reports an array of extreme and intense emotions that surpass what we now consider near-death experiences. Communication with the deceased, as well as the abundance of heavenly and bright light are quite similar to the patterns which we now are able to discern.

In the case of the description of Monchaux the comparisons to the patient who was suffering from what was then a bizarre and bizarre situation is very similar and very like the experiences that Charlier discovered. When considering the historical instances of NDE It might be a shock to learn to learn that French medical profession in the 17th century offers an abundance of information. However, with the conflicts, revolutions and turmoil that were taking place in France at the period, hypothermia cases as well as drowning, hanging and other dangers to life and limbs should not cause any surprise.

While both Monchaux and the authors of the Charlier's papers speculated about the medical reasons of the events they discussed, their explanations for blood rushes or trapped veins at best, speculation. In the past, the rising understanding of medical science and the growing necessity to record every medical anomaly and experience has resulted in increased understanding. This is why we're in perhaps the most fascinating position in history, as well as the experience of a near-death. In contrast to those who tend to dismiss miracles or other phenomena advancements in technology and medical technology have provided an abundance of information for researchers and others to explore the experiences of those who are near death.

Chapter 2: Worldwide Phenomena

If you're or are fascinated by the phenomenon of the near-death experience, then a fascinating aspect is the manner that different culture have described similar experiences. One of the leading researchers in studies of the culture of this topic is Gregory Sushan. Through his work, Sushan has examined accounts from five of the greatest civilizations that have shaped the history of humanity:

* Vedic India
* The Old as well as the Middle Kingdom Egypt
* Pre-Buddhist China
* Sumerian and Old Babylonian Mesopotamia
* Pre-Columbian Mesoamerica

When you take these cultures into consideration and incorporating these cultures, people might be surprised to learn about the widespread use of near-death experiences, the exact same process as the shamanic afterlife, as well as the spiritual journeys that souls be expecting. All across the various cultures that are in existence, the nine main aspects of the contemporary NDE are found in the instances from the past. Through analyzing these similarities Sushani has managed to affirm both the physiological and religious theories.

If you are looking for information on all the studies on anthropology and culture that have been conducted with regards to NDEs as well as the cultural distinctions that they bring, the Augustine study of 2003 is a good place to begin. In conclusion it is suggested that the content of NDEs doesn't change in significant ways. In reality, it's the character of the main people in the stories that alter. Instead of Jesus for instance people who were raised in the Hindu culture may encounter Yamaraja who is known as the Hindu King of Death. The minor differences in these stories show the wide spread of the fundamental tenets that comprise the NDE with minor modifications.

The study was published within The Journal of the American Society for Psychical Research in the year 1986, Satwant Pasricha and Ian Stevenson carried out research that looked into the details of sixteen instances in NDE that occurred in India. Despite the tiny sample size that they analyzed, Pasricha as well as Stevenson were in a position to draw connections in Indian as well as Western NDE events, though there were some distinctions. While American people might claim to be capable of seeing their own body from the distance, this isn't found in Indian reports. The idea of the journey to another realm is also a bit different in the sense that Indian reports typically contain an outside party who would take the person who died to an afterlife, where it would be realized that the mistake was not committed and the person could be able to wake up. This is different from American reports, where the deceased relatives play the function. The Western patient is usually returning due to the love of their life or an awareness of incomplete business, not because of the appearance of an error made by a clerk.

In determining the reason for the differences in Hindu stories and their commonly Western equivalents, the main explanation is usually the context of culture. When you are in the terrifying and confusing scenario that a near-death experience typically is, the necessity to establish an understanding and context on situations that are not familiar typically stems from the culture. We draw on our familiar stories as well as beliefs and religions to help us understand the utterly absurd. Through the use of the culture we have the most experience with people from all over the world are able to make understanding of their own circumstance by using what they know concerning the afterlife, and any journey that it may take.

Alongside Hindu theories of the near-death experience Sushani draws upon his knowledge from early Hebrew writers to enhance us understand. In the Jewish religion, the early people believed in heaven as three levels of the universe that included the heavens, Earth, and the underworld. Heaven was the exclusive domain that was the domain of God and angels. Humans would be a part of the middle world and the dead's souls would go through the third tier, which was known as the subterranean "She'ol." In addition, as well as the well-known tale of Daniel The Hebrew Scriptures also give us the tale about Elijah and his ascend to heaven. Reincarnation of Elijah in the form of Malachi is believed to be one of the indicators of the coming to the Messiah. The Bible explains that "reincarnation" in the sense of Elijah returning from a near-death experience, which was not a mystery with the early sects of Judaism. The people who practice Hasidic Judaism are invested in the belief that reincarnation is a reality, the extension and alternate form of which is discussed in the mysterious Kabbalah.

For the present Jewish people those who adhere to the strictest of beliefs have embraced the doctrine of Reincarnation, while non-orthodox adherents believe in the more metaphysical interpretation of an immortal soul. Whatever particular sect or variation of Judaism one believes in the notion of reincarnation as well as returning from death is an extremely important and central idea.

Another interesting culture that Sushani considers is traveling through East Asia. In the Tibetan Book of the Dead, Tibetan Book of the Dead could be thought of as an instruction manualthat informs readers about the journey from the live-world to the world of the dead. There is an intermediate stage that lasts for 49 days beginning immediately after the moment of death, and then transitioning to an entirely new body. Although it is primarily a philosophical framework in which the Tibetan Buddhists debate mortality and the meaning of life (rather than an account in actual terms of actual experiences) it is also a fascinating book. Book of the Dead is intriguing because it shows the interweaving of death-related rituals and the religious practice that was in existence prior to Buddhism, Bonism.

Contrary to other religions which focus on the death process, this one is also the way to reincarnation; the practice of reviving and reincarnation is inextricably tied to the religion as well as the beliefs of its practitioners.

As we study religious traditions from around the world and also personal accounts of history and the past, we realize the importance of the transition between life and death is in all religions. While many may dismiss the concept of a near-death experience as mere skepticism enormity and importance of similar experiences across the globe demands to be analyzed more deeply.

A Scientific Explaination?
As bizarre and confusing as near-death experiences may appear the advancements of medical technologies and research have made it clear that science is not satisfied with just observing these events. We are now looking for an explanation. By bringing

together all the theories that exist and suggesting explanations, the article of 2011 by Scientific American is a great base from which to begin.

The article starts by addressing the majority of what is recognized about the phenomenon. It is the fact that there exist a variety of common elements found in a variety instances. They include a feeling of dying and becoming dead as well as a feeling that the soul has left out of body is a journey towards an unlit shining light that points towards an alternate reality. While these feelings appear mysterious, scientists are now beginning to speculate about what causes them and how they can occur.

It's been determined that around three percent of the population in America United States has had a near-death experience, due to the findings of an earlier Gallup survey. If someone has an NDE but there are a few who are at risk of death as one study found up to half of them weren't in any real danger. However, the majority of individuals in question definitely believed themselves as being in danger. They were reported all over the nation, with evidence from the time of ancient Greece and even further back the recurrence of this phenomenon is a reason the reason why scientists would want to find a reason.

In an interview with the Scientific American, Dean Mobbs an neuroscientist at the University of Cambridge - provides his explanation of some of these experiences. He believes that a lot of the phenomena inherent to the experience of near death can be explained by the understanding of the biological basis of. Mobbs is in charge of the institution's Medical Research Council Cognition and Brain Sciences Unit and his work in collaboration and Caroline Watt of the University of Edinburgh has led to an extensive amount of knowledge regarding this area.

One of the areas that research studies focus on is the feeling of being as if one been dead. This feeling isn't restricted to NDEs however, research has revealed accounts of patients suffering from conditions like

Cotard (or "walking corpse syndrome") where patients are possessed by the belief that they've died. These types of cases typically are the result of traumatizing events such as the typhoid or multiple sclerosis and can affect the prefrontal cortex as well as the parietal cortex areas of the brain. This latter affects the process of focusing and the former is an issue when there is a mental disorders like schizophrenia. When taken together, they offer the patient a completely convincing sensation of dying. It is important to understand that the understanding of these disorders isn't complete However, the mechanism that causes the symptoms is not known. Mobbs is able to offer some possible explanations, such as patients are trying to comprehend the traumas they've endured, but with the brain in a position to conclude that it is dead.

Experiences of out-of-body are yet another element of NDE that is the subject of intense attention by researchers. The same thing happens when sleeping patterns are disrupted and occur right before bed and before awakening. A condition called sleep paralysis is the sensation of being in a state of paralysis while being aware of the world around you. According to reports, up to 40% of people suffer from this disorder, and it has been linked to vivid dreams and hallucinations. The hallucinations may leave patients feeling that they're outside of their own bodies , and seem to be floating. In 2005, researchers has shown that such experiences out of body experiences can be created artificially by activating stimulation of the right temporoparietal connection in the brain of a patient. This suggests to researchers that the inability to discern information from the senses during an NDE could fundamentally alter the way the patient perceives the external world. In the case of the previous research however, researchers could not provide specific details regarding near death experiences, or to fully confirm the existence of a connection between the two conditions.

There has been a range of ideas for people who are pondering the possibilities of NDE patients being said to be meeting relatives who have passed away. One of the comparisons drawn is the tendency for Parkinson's patients to experience visions of ghosts, people and other entities in the course of suffering from the condition. The reason for this is that the patients exhibit abnormal dopamine function. It is believed that a neurotransmitter within the brain can be capable of triggering hallucinations for patients.

Similar to those who have reported recalling memories from their past or reliving experiences, one idea that researchers have offered concerns the coeruleus locus. This is a part of the midbrain that releases noradrenaline. It is an inflammatory hormone that would normally be released when the sufferer is suffering from high levels of trauma. The locus coeruleus can be described as one of the brain regions that is closely linked to the mediating of memories and emotions within the mind and includes examples of the hypothalamus and the amygdala. Near-death experiences, as it's suggested they may be connected to the same neurological release.

One effect that can be reproduced through the use of medicines and even recreational substances includes the sensation of general euphoria that can be a powerful way to counteract the negative effects with an NDE. The research into the chemical reproduction of effects have included those caused by anesthetic ketamine. It is another drug that has been found to trigger hallucinations and experiences that are like the ones described in out-of-body experiences that are described by many people.

Ketamine is an injectable drug with similar effects as those observed in NDE

This happens by affecting the opioid system in the brain and the system is able to become active even without any drugs. Animals that have been attacked have experienced similar incidents as measured and this suggests that trauma could be the catalyst for triggering an ensuing chain of research-based suggestions.

A surprisingly infamous aspects of the near-death experience, which was discussed by Scientific American Magazine is the tendency of those experiencing the experience of a near-death experience to believe they are heading toward an intense white light. While researchers aren't able to give any precise explanation of the cause however, there is a possibility to suggest that tunnel vision that is a result of the loss of oxygen and blood flow may resemble a bright illumination in the eye. For people suffering from a severe case of anxiety or deficiency in oxygen levels, this phenomenon might be relevant.

Collectively, one suggestion from science that is offered to explain the effects that the body suffers in an NDE is based on the events that happen during normal brain functioning fails. Additionally the knowledge of this phenomenon has served as a tool for cultural preparation that teaches people what they can expect should they experience an encounter with death, effectively as a self-fulfilling prophecy.

According to Mobb's suggestion Mobb's suggestions, these results "provide the scientific basis for something that's been a part of paranormality." The combination of medical and chemical events that could occur at once could offer us a blueprint of what the human body will experience as it is close to death.

The wide range of ideas that are being offered and compared with the broad range of anecdotes and reports from a variety of people, coming to an exact conclusion about the scientific basis of the near-death experience is becoming more complicated than ever. Instead of offering an explanation of why medical science has assisted us to define the what, which is exactly what the body goes through after the time of a close encounter with death. The process of determining the exact cause is the next step.

Chapter 3: Angels And The Role Of Angels

If you think about the stories of those who've had the experience of a near-death experience there is a common theme that emerges: angels' presence in nearly every story. As we'll discover in the next chapter, stories range from abstract tales of glowing lighting to the classic portrayals of angels, as you could be able to see on the roof at the Sistine Chapel.

So, what exactly do we refer to as angels? It can be helpful to know that although angels are often considered to be a part of only Christian beliefsystem, similar creatures are present in a variety of religions. For both Zoroastrianism as well as Abrahamic faiths, such beings are typically described as gracious and compassionate beings capable of acting as intermediaries between the world and the afterlife, or as guardian figures that guard the believers.

Their roles also include safeguarding humanity. In the greater Christian canon (books like Paradise Lost), they were fighting against evil forces including demons. Angels have been given the responsibility of performing tasks and duties by God and others have been depicted in innocent, cherubs playing the harp while on clouds. Whatever kind of angel you can imagine, you can be sure that somebody has met them in an experience of near-death.

Due to their ubiquitous involvement in Western religions, and their equally important functions in a variety of Eastern religions It should come as no surprise that the sightings of and experiences with angels have been recorded throughout history. A survey carried out in the name of Time magazine placed belief in angels in Americans as 69% 46% of respondents believed they had a guardian angel who was watching over them. A poll conducted by Gallup found that 13 percent of Americans believed that they'd experienced an angel or like supernatural entity.

Although the amount of belief in angels among the modern Americans and similar entities that are found in different religions and cultures doesn't provide absolute proof of near-death experiences, it can aid in understanding the beliefs of those who meet celestial beings during these instances. The fact that the belief has become so commonplace and that the knowledge of the role for angels so obvious can provide us with a better understanding on the reason why people are able to see everything from glowing lights to robed figures as a similar being.

Given the general belief in angels and the varying interpretations and understanding of exactly what they're the angels that are featured in numerous NDE accounts shouldn't come as a shock.

Celebrities" Near Death Experiences"
Before we look at the near-death experiences of different people, it may be beneficial to review a number of examples of famous people who have an account to share. Contrary to the people who became famous due to an NDE These famous people have a unique perspective to the events.

The pop superstar Ozzy Osbourne might seem an unlikely candidate for an NDE.

Ozzie Osbourne - Image source: Wikipedia

But this English singer "died twice" after a motorbike accident that left him in an induced coma for 8 days. After slipping on leaves , and being thrown off the bars of the handle when the bike crashed over the rider and crushed his chest. His bodyguards tried to assist, offering CPR as well as other emergency treatment, Ozzy stopped breathing twice. After waking up from the coma Osbourne said that his experience was very difficult. At times, he was in no clue who he was, or the place he was. He is able to clearly remember an intense light that emerged through the darkness.

In his presentation to people, he claims that he witnessed "no trumpets blaring and nobody sporting a beard of white," Ozzy's story is like other accounts that are abstract. For someone who was famous for his alcohol and drug drinking habits, Osbourne used his biography to discuss how these events eventually forced him to confront with his own life and "grow into."

One name that is more well-known to those who are older could be Jane Seymour. The actress who appeared in the shows on television like "Dr Quinn, Medicine Woman" and films like Somewhere in Time opposite Christopher Reeves and was 36 years old of age when she experienced her near-death incident. Jane suffered a severe influenza. To aid in recovery, she received an injection of penicillin from her doctor. However, the actress was very sensitive to penicillin and it only made her condition more severe, enough to cause her to be close to death.

Jane Seymour - Image source: Wikipedia

Seymour describes the moment in which she "literally removed herself from her body." She recounts the feeling of being able to gaze at the surrounding area, only to see her lying in the bed and observe how doctors attempted to revive her. In the upper part of the room she floated over them, and watched as medical team held her body onto the bed. When they began pushing the needles through her arm, they needed to hold her tight.

Additionally she will be able to remember her entire life "flashing before her eyes". With a full and exciting life She says she is not thinking about Emmys or other awards however, she is determined to live and to return to the care of her children. Then she began to discuss her thoughts with God and said, "If you're there, God is there, and if you do exist and I can survive I will never let your name as a slur again." Jane Seymour died for approximately 30 seconds, she remembers, then suddenly returned to her body. She awoke.

Another actress who has recalled getting close to dying was Sharon Stone. The lead in the film The Basic Instinct, Stone has told of how a brain ache resulted in her being confronted by an intense white light. An artery that runs through the middle of her skull had been shattered by an ailment that caused internal bleeding. She talked to Katie Couric about her experience and the road it placed her on:

Sharon Stone Source image Wikimedia

"When it struck my head," Stone recalls, "I felt as if I was shot in the head. This is the only way that I can truly describe the feeling." It was a medical emergency was the catalyst that led Stone on her journey, which she called "a genuine trip ... one that brought me to places in the present and beyond, that affected me in such a way that my life is never the same ... I am no longer scared of dying, and I'm able to share with others that it's a wonderful event and that death is a blessing. Not that you have to be a martyr, but when death does come to you, which it will, it's a beautiful and glorious thing. This huge swirl of white light was descending upon me, and I was poof! It was like I took off into this magnificent bright, bright white light. I began to look around and meet some of my buddies."

Then, as fast as it started, Sharon found herself back in the room. Although she may not have felt the need to make a change in her life in the same way as Ozzy Osbourne, she has been able to talk about the experience as a profound and significant event throughout her career.

One of the most compelling instances of the Hollywood celebrity experiencing a life-changing near death experience is the tale of Gary Busey. At one time, he was considered to be one of the world's most notorious party-goers and someone who could be deemed in out of control Gary Busey was known for his constant battle with alcohol and drugs which eventually led his wife to call his name "Gary abusing".

Garey Busey - Image source Wikipedia

Yet, Gary had supernatural and life-altering experiences at least three times in his lifetime. He was close to dying three times in the form of overdose from a prescription drug, another following the diagnosis of cancer but most important most importantly, a motorbike accident that took place at the border of New Mexico. Gary was driving through Albuquerque in 1988 without helmet. The bike fell off in 1988 and Busey was thrown headfirst over the curb along the road. He was taken to the hospital, and then placed on the operating table. Busey remembers a near death moment as doctors struggled in vain to spare his life.

In this moment he recalled being in the presence of angels. Instead of the traditional versions that are often used on the Christmas card, Busey informs his biographers about angels simply being huge balls of light carrying with them only warmth and unconditional love nature. After recovering from the accident Busey thought about his experience prior to death. He decided to commit all of his time to Jesus and has since become a renowned speaker at numerous Christian gatherings and celebrations. In contrast to his addiction-ridden background Gary Busey's NDE transformed him into a god-fearing person.

Chapter 4: The Real World Examples Of The Near Death Experience

Alongside being aware of the medical, cultural and historical roots of the phenomenon of near-death experiences The most effective way to learn more about it is to study the experiences of those who were involved in these types of incidents.

In the following pages, you'll be able read about the range and depth of of the NDEs people have had to endure. These 10 case studies were chosen as each case study brings a distinct perspective to the table.

Before you decide on your own thoughts about the experience that others have had, go through the accounts of those who have shared their experiences to understand the whole details of the near-death incident.

Mary Neal, Dr. Mary Neal
The journey begins with the true stories of NDEs with a self-proclaimed skeptical. The Dr. Mary Neal is now regularly appearing on talk shows, and is her own well-loved book

on her experiences. She has a story to tell on On the Today show, she was at one time an agnostic.

At one point, the doctor. Neal was simply a practicing spinal surgeon in Wyoming. She could not describe herself as someone who could "claim to be especially religiose." Being a physician she was who was used to having a precise understanding of the issues before her and was able to heal patients that had gone before her.

The situation would alter during the fateful kayaking experience. Doctor. Neal was paddling her kayak in an eddy when the flow began to roar. A surge took her off the water's surface and forced her to the bottom of the river. After the incident, she sustained two broken legs, and started to experience major problems in her lung. In the water Dr. Neal was drowning. It was pouring into her body and she struggled to breathe. With two legs broken and a kayak wedged between her, and the air that hung above the water, getting back to the safety zone was becoming less likely. Mary Neal began to die.

She describes her experience on the brink of death as being around 20 minutes. During this time, she realized of her imminent death. The kayaking guides along with her have confirmed her report, confirming the length of time in when they tried to figure out what happened and then tried to help the doctor.

But Mary did not simply drown. At this point she clearly recalls being taken to another area. Many people think drowning as a violent fight, Mary Neal recalls a tranquil journey, surrounded by bright lights and angels "exploding with pure love." Although she can not recall any specific characters appearing before her, she can recall the overwhelming feeling being in the presence the angels Jesus as well as God.

"They appeared to be a kind of compassion," she explained on The Today show. "even although that's the word that is not used as an adjectival." As she stood before the religious leaders the realization dawned upon Mary that this wasn't the best time to go to the grave. Mary was informed by the spirits that a terrible tragedy was going to occur to her and she would have to return to the realm where the dead live. In particular she was told that her son, who was then nine years old, was going to die, and that it would not happen prior to her own death. She was expected to provide support to her family during this tragic time. Mary was revived. She was assisted by guides and others who were with her and was able to get through the incident. However, it wasn't without cost. The patient would spend a month in a hospital recovering, and then was forced to spend another six months off from work, and be in wheelchair. As a physician who is highly aware of the very low chance of her survival and, surprisingly enough the more fortunate she was.

The incident changed the course of events for Dr. Mary Neal. Like we said she was a person who could have said she was a skeptic or an agnostic. Today, she is far from that. She came to believe she was Jesus who helped her out of the depths of the sea and allowed her to survive. In light of these experiences, she was inspired to write a novel, which was published in 2012. The title was To Heaven And Back The book tells the reader about her complex and life-affirming tale. She has been featured on numerous television shows as well as in numerous print publications, spreading message about her near-death incident that transformed her life.

The story doesn't stop there. According to visions she had during the NDE Mary's son died in death. After ten years of the incident, when she returned to be with her son, he passed away in a car crash at the age 19 and was struck by a motorist from Maine who was using cellphone.

For Mary the tragedy has only confirmed what transpired to her under the water. As the final, devastating confirmation that it was a traumatic event, it has been a traumatic experience for Mary more than just reaffirming the faith she has in God. It gave her an opportunity to be warned and a glimpse of what might transpire this event has given Mary an extra year to treasure her bond and her husband, even though she knew that only coming to one end.

Crystal McVea

As we've seen in the case of the Dr. Mary Neal, near deaths are usually abrupt and unplanned. They may provide us with an insight into the nature of world we may not have thought of. In trying to explain the creatures that encounter during this type of incident, the details of the event can become difficult to quantify and hard to connect to other individuals. One person who is more than others to convey a near-death experience to other people is Crystal McVea.

The background of Crystal McVea's is not atypical enough. Growing up within Oklahoma, Crystal was, to the extent that she was she was a normal woman. Although she was an orthodox Christian however, her faith was slipping away in the same way to that of the late Dr. Neal. She wouldn't have considered herself among the most passionate of her acquaintances or neighbours.

The situation changed in a surprising moment in. As Mary Neal encountered death out in the wild, Crystal McVea was in hospital in 2009. After undergoing a standard procedure to combat the pancreatitis condition, Crystal fell into complete respiratory collapse. It is a serious disease in which the body ceases breathing after the lungs have started to fail and stop to circulate air throughout the body.

Of all the locations to be prone to an illness that could be life-threatening Operating tables are probably among many people's most preferred places. When a patient appeared to die in the course of a regular medical procedure doctors were on the scene to help ensure that Crystal breathing again and to save her. After being in such a dire and dangerous situation Crystal had walked into the operating room hoping to recover but instead, she was confronted to face with the life beyond the living.

On Fox News' Fox News show Fox and Friends that later became part of The Huffington Post, Crystal McVea was able recount the experience that her failed procedure led her on. As soon as she shut her eyes in the hospital recalled her awakening in heaven. "I had angels I had God and I dropped to my knees the front of him," she told the host on the show. She suggested that her transition to the new realm began when she was asleep at the table, rather than when respiratory arrest started.

As opposed to other encounters that allow people to remember exactly the length of time they were in different locations and precisely where they went the entire trip is somewhat more intangible. One area where we can see an eerie resemblance however, is the manner in which McVea responds to people who seek a description of God.

Crystal claims the idea that "human words" are not able to describe what she experienced. This is in line with the things other people have stated including Mary Neal, but people like Ozzy Osbourne as well - making the abstract and mystical nature of the creatures that are encountered during near-death experiences. Mary Neal describes seeing an enthralling light and feeling overwhelmed by the sensation of being in the presence of a divine being.

These feelings help to create the picture of what it would be like to have been in that moment with Crystal McVea in that moment. In her words the senses of her were overpowered and heightened and the first time ever felt sensations taking over her. She recalls "an incredible brightness the brightness that you could taste, feel listen to, touch, and smell that filled me with joy. It's not as if my five senses were present, but that I had 500 or more senses."

In this location McVea remembers the person she believed to be God asking her two times if she'd like to return to the home where the dead live. Each time, she replied that she would rather stay in this wonderful and new area. Despite being a skeptical person, Crystal's faith was renewed. "All my life I was doubting," she says, "and consequently, to shut my eyes and stand in front of the one who created not only this universe but also of me, I've never would want to go away from this."

But, following her second request that she wanted to remain, Crystal McVea was returned to her body. When she left however, she claims that God eliminated her guilt and shame, "freeing" her. After returning to her own body awoke up to discover how complicated the situation was and the calamity that occurred to her as she had travelled away.

Similar to as Dr. Neal, Crystal McVea is now saying that her incident has altered the way she views her faith. Being with her own God It seemed that it was enough to rekindle the faith that had diminished prior to the events at the hospital. Another time, the experience of a near-death incident has helped to bring someone who was distracted or depressed by spirituality to their faith.

Like many others who have been close to dying and had life-changing, Crystal McVea decided that her personal story was one she wanted to share with world. Along with the numerous interviews she did on news channels and the stories published on The Huffington Post and other publications, McVea published a book in 2013. The title was Waking Up In Heaven The book travels some distance to describe the exact path that she went on as her breathing stopped function, and helps others understand more about the experience she had.

Veronika Barthel

While many focus on the positives of an NDE and the manner that it can be used to affirm the belief in an omnipotent being, the experience can be negative at times. Although we've already examined situations where people have met angels and other divine beings but there were also occasions that saw people who were close to death start seeing an alternate view of their afterlife. One of these people is named Veronika-UlrikeBarthel. In contrast to many other individuals on this listing, her story is not in a book. Instead, she has put her story online for the world to view. As if she was threatening other people, her story is more sinister than the one we've seen before.

The near-death experience of Veronika occurred when she was just 22 years old, however the story started much earlier. When she spoke to "Hands For Charity," the German site "Hands to Charity" she recounts the events that resulted in her near-death experience.

Her mother was only 18 year old Veronika Barhel was soon able to find her new stepfather. But, he soon began to dislike her. Veronika is able to connect the rejection and this relationship to numerous negative events of her young life. At her five years of age and was a regular at the church. It was at this time, she suggests that she decided to accept Jesus as a part of her life. This was particularly helpful in lonely times. When she was feeling down she would find herself praying for comfort.

At times, she would lay on her bed, crying. She was not allowed to cry before her stepfather. When she would break into tears in front of him the punishment would be an even more severe punishment. At the age at seven years, Veronika ran away from her home, attempting to escape and shelter at the home of her grandmother.

In the wake of the many horrible childhood experiences, she recollects falling out of belief in God and losing faith in the God who allowed these events to occur to her.

The depression she suffered eventually resulted in 3 suicides. At her lowest, Veronkia was able to revive her faith and found her inner strength to accept her stepfather's guilt for his actions and the way he had treated her when she was a child. In this situation that Veronika was after she was so close to dying.

The 13th of June 1981, she was on her way home from an event. It began to pour as well as her belt was left behind, stuck inside the locked door, inaccessible to her. In the blink of an eye, it turned extremely bright inside the vehicle. A lightning bolt hit the car during the storm, sending Veroinika into a terribly dangerous situation when her vehicle and she were swept away by the flashing illumination. Veroinika began screaming.

It's at this point that she remembers getting rid of her body. She observed her from the outside sitting in her chair with her hands burned and still clinging to the wheel. From there, she walked swiftly through a tunnel, rising over her like the shape of a canyon. She did not touch anything and is in awe of the words to adequately describe the terrifying situation where she was watching her. When she came to the final point of the tunnel Veronika was standing before the massive gate. The entrance was engraved with"the words "Welcome into Hell."

When she enters those gates, Veronika recollects being chased by demons across into the world of. Contrary to other NDE experiences, thoughts of angels and heaven appear quite different from what Veronika experienced. In her surroundings there were people screaming with fervent requests for help from Jesus. She was not able to help those in need as she was taken by the police through the streets.

Although it may seem like to be the complete opposite of experiences that others have experienced There is a resemblance in the manner in which Veronika describes the people she encountered during that time. Similar to McVea's and Neal's descriptions about angels, Veronika is unable to articulate in exact terms her descriptions of those that guided her through the terrifying surroundings. They resembled soldiers. were able to lead her in a crowd of screaming people in distress. Breathing became difficult and a pungent smell filled her nose. There was an lava lake, full of curses and apprehensions people.

The walls were dotted with demons. They were armed with spears and they'd smash them in the bodies of those who were condemned. They soon began to sink in with their spears Veronika. She had never felt pain like it. All over her body her nerves were screaming in pain. On the floor, snakes crawled across snakes, with the floor appeared to be writhing around. Even to this day the memories of the location makes your stomach hurt. Veronika Barthel was confronted with the terror and fear that she had never heard of.

Then, a few hours later she awoke. Instead of waking up at a medical facility or doctor's office, she discovered that she was in the presence Jesus. The voice he spoke to her, she recalls as being the "loveliest" she'd ever heard. Similar to others, she recalls an "unimaginable luminosity." He escorted the woman back into her own body and left her with the clear instruction to tell what she'd witnessed.

Then she awoke and began screaming "I had died and was in Hell". She was driving to the house of her grandmother. The lightning had gone out and she was back from the brink of dying. The neighborhood was filled with people in their pajamas gathered in front of the vehicle, shocked of the incident they witnessed. As they began to examine the melted plastic on the vehicle there was a clear indication that the car had suffered a terrible accident to the young lady. She sought medical attention and was eventually able to recover but the memories of the incident remain with her for the rest of time since.

It was not the first occasion that Veronika was confronted with death. Her website recounts the same experience in Frankfurt when she was driving to the house of her grandmother. Although she doesn't have the same reach as other NDE memories and hasn't had the same public appearances as numerous others have done but she is left with a strong determination to share her story to everyone who is willing to be willing to listen. As a woman who suffered terrible childhoods seeing this glimpse of the realm of the afterlife has helped her discover a new faith this world and she's made a promise to assist others in escaping the hell she witnessed.

Howard Storm

We've talked about skeptical and skeptics as well as people who had doubted their faith in the wake of an near-death experience, maybe none of them were as determined to their denial of faith than Howard Storm. A man who claimed to be an "double atheist" his experience with a universe that was not his personal beliefs was enough to alter his beliefs about the supernatural and spiritual. To discover the whole background that led to Howard Storm, it can be beneficial to trace the story back to an earlier time prior to the incident that was when Howard was at the forefront of his belief in the atheist religion.

Howard was self-described as a "know-it-all teacher at a college." He was an instructor at the age of 27 and was a lecturer in Northern Kentucky University on the topic of Fine Art. In the early days the lack of faith was one of his key characteristics, with his skeptical nature and lack of faith being one of the main characteristics that he identified himself with. This was evident when he organized an excursion for his students, which included an entire three-week trip with his students to the best galleries Europe offers.

After the tour had was finally in Paris, Storm decided to take a break in his hotel room and get some rest after spending the day studying some of the most famous artworks, as well as instructing his students on the meanings and stories that artists concealed in their art. It was the day that ended of the tour and the instructor was already anticipating having a much-needed break and take a break for some time to rest.

However, his rest was not. In a tense pain his wife and a close student watched at in disbelief when he bent his back and yelled. He was taken to the hospital and found out that he had an extremely serious illness. According to his own words, "I had a perforation of my stomach's small intestine which is called duodenum." It was like he'd been shot. When he began screaming and writhing it was soon clear that he'd require surgery. Not able to locate the ideal doctor, Storm was seemingly confined to his extreme pain.

He was put in the room while a doctor was requested. Although he was prescribed strong painkillers, he had to take care of himself. Without much that physicians could accomplish without the proper surgeon, his situation was looking bleak. In the bed, awake as he reminisces about the events and events that afflicted him. After saying goodbye to his wife and sending his final message before he went to sleep, he collapsed into unconsciousness.

The exorcism started. He was in the hospital bed looking at his body, but , as he said, "I refused to believe that it could be me." Then he heard voices calling him from outside the room. They spoke in non-accented English It was quite different from the French which he'd come to believe he would receive. He tried to communicate with his wife, and everyone else that he could see inside the room to determine if there were voices but they couldn't hear the voice of him. The pain had gone away, but the voices in across the hall were calling to him. They were requesting for him to follow them.

When he arrived at the entrance, Howard questioned whether they were hospital personnel. He was in need of surgery, he said that no one could locate the right doctor ease the discomfort. "We know everything about you," one said. "We've had our eyes on you for a long time. It's time to leave. Get ready." Howard walked with them, walking farther and further along the hallway, which became dimmer and more dark. The light started to fade away from the room. Even with the distance they had walked He did not get tired and then began to question what was the reason why pain seemed unaffected by his body.

The corridor became dark and Howard began to become more lost and confused, he began asking questions of his guides. "Where do we go?" he asked. "Where are the doctors?" The guides hushed him and tried to stifle his concerns, but then they rushed to the far end of the hallway, shrouded in darkness. Unwilling to move further, Howard dug in his heels and stood his ground.

They tried to push him, and pulled him away. They seemed desperate to push him to the far end of the room in order to keep him from whatever light was. Howard later explains that Howard later explains the incident, they "had an intense fight, which ended up with them killing me. They did this slow and with great enthusiasm. The majority of them were cutting and tearing me. The whole thing went on for quite a while. They also did various things to humiliate and hurt me that I never discuss." Howard Storm was stuck. The strange location was unknown to Howard Storm. It was completely contrary to everything believed he was aware of. The self-proclaimed status of an "double atheist" was unraveling in front of his eyes. Everything he that he believed in was a mess. The pain was getting unbearable. The fight between his previous guides was intensifying. They were ripping into his body. And then, in the distance an unassuming voice spoke at him "Pray God." God."

Howard was thinking about his youth and what Howard remembered about his childhood. The prayers returned to him through the air. He began to say his version of the Lord's Prayer. His guides were furious. They were furious, shouting at him, yelling that they had no God and that Howard must remain silent as they went about their work. They yelled, but Howard did not stop praying. When he had reached the conclusion of the Lord's Prayer, he turned to other prayers which he could recall. In a frantic recitation, shouting out the prayers of his guide, his followers became in awe. They fled away.

Howard Storm was left lying on the floor of the dark corridor. He was sure that his torturers were gone however, he also knew that they did not go far. In a state of agony He began to think at his past. He looked back at his life to the point where he concluded that he'd lived the most "crummy" existence. "Whatever it was that life should be all about, I did not get the point," he thought. "What I received was exactly what I earned and those who attacked me were just similar to me. They were my friends. And now I'll be with them for the rest of my life."

His thoughts reverted to his childhood, and thoughts of Jesus returned into the front of his thoughts. In the midst of this thought in his mind and yelling out in the darkness. A flash of light appeared. Howard recognized it as Jesus and "His arms were extended to me, and he touched me and my body was healed and was put back together. He embraced me with love that I didn't know was there." Howard was shown the wrong way to live. An alcohol drinker and an adultererer He began looking back in shame at what he'd committed. Howard was able to ask Jesus whether he was in heaven. "No" is the simplest answer, since Howard was set to be returned in his own body.

Howard Storm woke up in the hospital, and from that point on, he was determined to live his life in a new way. The event had transformed Howard's life. Similar to Veronika was, it required an adventure to the deepest darkest places to allow Howard to rekindle his faith. Howard was treated for his illness, and he was able to make a complete recovery. Following his recovery, Howard did what many patients who've experienced near-death experiences do: write an autobiography.

Instead of merely recollections, Howard's tale is one that he prefers to consider as a kind of redemption. There is no more adultery or the drinking. After his encounter with these strange guards who Howard thinks were demons his near-death experience an epochal Parisian afternoon was enough to alter the character of this committed "double atheist."

Don Piper
Contrary to those who have been changed to spirituality because of their near-death experiences Some people discover that the experience confirms what they believe. Similar to the self-fulfilling prophecy previously mentioned, people who have faith in God are frequently presented with what they believe to be truthful. One example of this is the story for Don Piper.

Don's story starts with a sigh of relief. When he attended a pastor's meeting in the beginning of January in 1989, he was pleased to learn that the event ended sooner than he anticipated. Don Piper was a busy person. As the associate pastor at his church, he'd been appointed recently as an education minister in the Houston region. If he could get home early, it could mean he could take a few extra minutes while organising his busy schedule. In an interview with CBN.com His mind was thinking about the night ahead and the reality that he was scheduled to preach at three times on the next Sunday morning.

Instead of returning home to work on his agenda But Don Piper would be met by a different set of circumstances. He returned home from the retreat centre by a well-known route. As he crossed a bridge over an eddy there was water from both sides. The road was a long and high-altitude road and that crossing over the bridge would be tiring but crucial aspect of the drive to home. According to Don recalls, the bridge was closing in front of him of the bridge and a tractor trailer truck "crossed through the central stripe and struck my car head-on."

Instead of a simple crash, the car smashed across the front of Don's tiny Ford escort. The car was completely crushed and Don was severely injured and suffered a fatal injury and died. "When I was struck by a car," he remembers, the deceased received the honor of being "instantly taken" to the gates of heaven. Then, Don was no longer in his vehicle, which is what he calls "an instantaneous event." He was in the company of familiar faces.

The faces that surrounded him were all familiar. "I didn't meet anyone I didn't recognize," he recalls. "They were family members and friends that had passed away in high school. they were teachers, they were people I'd seen and knew for a long time who were awe-inspiring." The entire group of individuals were resurfacing from his past and, as Don recalls, "They were smiling; they were welcoming me I was being welcomed by them as they were on the verge of guiding me through the gate to heaven."

From the distance far beyond his family and friends, Don could see a massive gate out in the distance. He described it as an "magnificent structure," saying that it looked as if it "had been created from mother-of pearl." In the gate Don could see a stunning illumination. It was one of them. Don declared that "I cannot imagine what it would look like in a human body. It's possible that it's in a celestial body since it was so bright." As with the other people who have been through an NDE in which putting words to the sounds and sights becomes more and more abstract. Don even recalls the music he was able to hear, and describes it as "that of an actual angelic, heavenly choir."

"In the end even as incredible as the sights were, the sound was even more impressive," Don remembers. "I was able to hear thousands of songs of praise." The accounts of sensory overload are similar to the experiences of others. He goes on to say, "You could sense this the hum of wings floating all over you, as if you were being ministered by angels and were watching the whole thing."

And in other areas, things weren't as enjoyable. Dick Onerecker, a fellow pastor from Kline in Texas was found on the highway alongside Don's body. Another participant at the conference was on the same route to home and was on the scene of the accident few minutes after. Medical personnel arrived and informed Don that Don was dead.

Dick states that he felt "compelled not to move and pray for his friend," but it didn't end there. The feeling was "impressed upon me with a great force and urgently to pray for Don." In the face of Don at risk, there was nothing Dick could do. However, according to his account that he walked over to the spot of the accident , and describes there was "great physical injury to the exterior." Then, Dick placed his hands on the body of his friend and "began to pray for the body of his friend."

To Don Piper, his journey started as soon as the war had ended. A moment later, standing in front of a magnificent light at the between the gate immediately he was back by the wrecked motorcar along the highway, gazing upwards at the bottom of the tarp that initial responders put onto his body. He was able to recall his shock at the scene, and thought, "I'm in the dark and I'm singing. I'm holding my hand. I'm wondering "What's going on?" In the distance, Dick had been quietly singing.

Don Piper was taken to Herman Hospital in Houston. Even though it seemed like a risk however, the doctors were able to find no internal or head injuries. However, the majority of bones inside his body was damaged or broken. Both his arm as well as his legs on his left were totally broken, requiring the reconstruction and replaced. In the midst of his broken and battered body, and looking through the discomfort, Don was only struck by the memories of what he'd seen during the time following the collision.

Despite the thoughts that swarm his mind, and the constant sensation that he wanted to return, Don pulled through with the help of a lot in physical therapy. He underwent numerous operations and, on two occasions the lingering infection was close to ending his life. He credits his recovery due to the assistance, support and prayers that he received from his friends and relatives. "I prefer to say that I returned due to popularity," he said. "People asked me to return from the heavens gates. They prayed for me from death's doorstep. I'm here because people prayed to God to allow the reason for me being here."

Although many have been blessed after a near-death incident but to Don Piper it was a issue of confirmation. While still a pastor, but not as charismatic as he was in the past, Don continues to spread his message, and more convinced than ever before of the truthfulness of his statements.

Colton Burpo

In reading the accounts of people who've had the experience of a near-death experience It is not unusual to see people become bored and bored. Many of the stories that follow similar patterns, and with a large number of the victims having similar lives after the event, the inference to an agenda or motive to the accounts is not unusual.

Colton Burpo's tale is a bit different. Although the majority of stories we read about come of adults Colton is a young child when he was close to dying. Furthermore is that he was young when he spoke to reporters and news organizations. Instead of having his narrative be influenced by cynicism or the age of his interviewer the Colton account as unique and fascinating in its own right.

Most of the stories put in this book will include several paragraphs devoted to their background and experiences leading up to the event we want to talk about. This cannot be the case for Colton Burpo. He was only four years old at the time his appendix ruptured, Colton was not averse to much in terms of experience or interest in or acceptance of any particular religion. Like many four-year-olds Colton was more preoccupied with the coming school year than his own soul. After being rushed to the hospital his story is beginning to line up with many other accounts.

After being taken to surgery, doctors needed to react quickly in order to save Colton's life. An appendix rupture could be life-threatening and medical personnel were already feeling the strain as they tried to rescue Colton. After repairing the injury within the body and stitch him up, they sewed the wound and hoping for the most favorable outcome. The patient was admitted to a hospital for recovery and then slept under the effects of anaesthetic. His parents were present all the time and when he finally woke up, his primary concern was to tell a story about the things he saw.

For Colton the procedure was not just an instance of getting blacked out. In the two hours were spent at the table of the surgeon, Colton had an account to relate. Colton, a young man, spoke to his parents, telling them the various religious figures that he encountered during the journey. In addition the boy remembers meeting relatives and friends who passed away in the the previous year. While the procedure was in progress the father of Colton walked to another area and started to pray. This was an image that Colton recalled experiencing during an out of body experience. Perhaps most intriguing there were two details that Colton was able to relay to others.

Colton Burpo remembers meeting his baby sister when he was under the knife of a doctor. The parents of Colton had never informed his son of the miscarriage Colton's mother was suffering from. They never had mentioned the child they lost, however Colton insists on talking about his baby sister who he not had the chance to meet. Additionally, Colton made oblique references to a man he called "Pop." "Pop" appeared to be an 18-year-old man. Colton provided his account to his parents, however they couldn't figure out the person he was speaking about. When the family finally got at home did Colton capable of identifying Pop from an older family picture. It was his paternal grandfather.

According to Fox News, Colton's father stated that "we were sure he didn't make the story up, since Colton could tell us what was happening in a different part in the hospital. It was the first time even Sonja was there in that small room being a mess to God."

In contrast to other patients who have experiences religious beliefs, have gained a lot of knowledge about the various interpretations of heaven that are based on culture and even discovered the phenomenon of near-death experiences Colton's story isn't suffused with this baggage. Contrary to other accounts included in the book Colton's story may be the one least stained by cynicism or doubt.

Colton Burpo made a complete recovery. Despite his close encounter with death, he's recovered enough to hold interviews to his parents and to be asked questions about the incident. A footnote in the story concerns his father. Although many are eager to publish a book after NDE, Colton was obviously incapable of doing this.

In the end, his father was able to take over the writing duties and wrote the book in his name. Therefore anyone who wants to learn more about the life about Colton Burpo can look up the book Heaven Is For Real, which tells the story of the boy in relation by his dad.

Ben Breedlove

After having read the story of Colton Burpo, the perspective of the younger generation could be something you'd like to understand more about. Enter Ben Breedlove. The near-death experience the young man is able to remember is not just fascinating because of his age Ben was just a teenager at the time his fame was born, but also because of the manner that he decided to share his personal story. With stories that span the entirety of his life Ben recorded his experiences and uploaded videos on the popular video sharing website YouTube. You can check them out yourself or read them to get a quick overview of the reasons why Ben's story was fascinating to so many.

Based on his own story, Ben was a Texas teenager who was a swindler three times. He was born with a risky heart condition, the 18 year old Austin native has spoken about hypertrophic cardiomyopathy as well as the way it transformed his lifestyle. The condition caused one region of the heart to be more thick than the others, making it more difficult for the muscle to circulate blood a proper way.

The most recent health-related scare was on the 6th of December 2011. After he collapsed at school, the medical personnel who arrived utilized a defibrillator in order to revive the patient. In the wake of this event, Ben put together a two-part YouTube series titled "This Is My Story." After the series was released the series has amassed nearly 1 million views.

Ben's unique method of telling stories may be foreign to those who expect an talk or confessional. His story is written down on notecards that he holds one after the next. One of his videos involves his telling the audience about the moment at the age of four, that his first attempt at dying.

The incident was described by Ben while being transported to the medical facility on a stretcher Ben recalls that "there was a huge bright light in the sky above my head ... I was unable to figure out what it was, due to the brightness. I said to my mother"Look at the glowing light'. I pointed it up. She told me she couldn't find anything." As he continues to play his cards and telling us "There was no lighting in this room. I couldn't keep my eyes off of it. And I couldn't resist a smile. I was not worried whatsoever, and nothing else did."

One of the things in the videos that affect a lot of viewers is the look at Ben's face while he relays his tale. When each card is removed, Ben's expression changes from serious expression and a wide smile. "I can't even begin to explain the tranquility, the peace it was" the writer writes "I will never forget that experience or the day."

Similar to others who have experienced the experience of a near-death and experienced this kind of abstract experience of calm and peace is one that they remember about their journey in the spirit world. Although doctors may suggest the brain is trying to comprehend the current circumstances, those who've experienced an NDE are steadfast in the events they experienced.

Ben's videos continueto tell of the second time was close to death. In the summer of 2011 Ben was admitted in the hospital for routine tonsil surgery , as do many teens. But Ben's illness complicated things and led him to cardiac arrest. "It is a wonder they saved me," he says in his video. "I was afraid to die, and am SO grateful that I did not."

Ben's third and last near-death experience also took place in 2011. According to the card, "I really thought to myself"This is it. "I'm going to die." Ben recalls what was on his mind during the event as he recalls being in a peaceful white room. There were no walls , and Ben recalls feeling "that the same calm feeling that I experienced when I was just 4." He clearly remembers being with one of his most fav artists, each "wearing an extremely nice costume," thinking to himself, "Damn, we look great."

Looking back at the time he was in this location, he recalls an overwhelming feeling of joy and warmth. "I did not want to leave," Breedlove wrote on his cards "I wanted to never wake up." The last card was one that laid out Ben's view of the things he'd observed and experienced. "Do your beliefs in Angels and God?" Breedlove wrote in the last card in the video. He concluded with the words, "I do."

Ben Breedlove passed away a just a few hours after. Since his death his films have been viewed many times and the legacy of Ben Breedlove has grown expanded. Along with the national media attention through CBS and Fox the rapper spoke of on the clip (Kid Cudi) came out to thank Ben for his support and family. While many of the people on this list have gone on to write books and share their newly converted gospel with renewed enthusiasm, Ben was denied this chance. Instead his videos are available for free viewing online and his legacy to humanity will come from his own story.

Ian McCormack

While all of the incidents that we have talked about in the past have occurred in America The near-death incident isn't a phenomenon that is only found in the US. Ian McCormack was born in London and grew up in Australia. In 1982 at the age of Ian was just 26, He was divers within the Indian Ocean. As a young, adventurous man, he took an excursion to Mauritius and had decided to go for some lobster diving. In the course of his dive however, he was struck by a jellyfish in a box. The most toxic species on the planet one touch from these animals can cause death in less than four minutes. At the point that the ambulance arrived at Ian He was completely immobilized. Another complication of this toxic poison necrosis was already beginning to enter the bone marrow of Ian.

Ian McCormack's near-death incident occurred during the journey into the hospital. In an ambulance, Ian was positioned on a stretcher while they made their way to medical facilities and recounts his life flashing in front of his eyes. Prior to these events, Ian would have classified himself as an agnostic. He was skeptical about whether there was any specific faith and was not sure about what would happen following the death. As he lay in the rear of an ambulance slowing dying, Ian recalls seeing a vision of his mother, the sole member of his family who could be described as Christian. She was praying for him.

During the mother's prayer, she urged her son to pray to God from the depths of his soul. God as she promised him, will hear the prayer and accept his sins and lack of faith. Uncertain of the specific prayers, Ian called out for God in the event that He existed to prove to him the truth of them. Ian was able to recall that the Lord's Prayer and began to repeat the prayer.

After arriving to the hospital doctors immediately set to work. They brought McCormack to the hospital and started providing him with the anti-toxins that were developed to counteract jellies' poison. They were in a losing battle, however. After a few minutes, Ian's pulse had stopped and his body lay in the bed, dead.

This is the period that McCormack is able to recall the most vividly. Despite the acuity of his memory, his writings in books and interviews clearly show that he was unsure exactly where he was. He tried reaching out, but realized that he could not grasp anything. When he tried to place his hands on the side of his body, they moved right through. The reason, Ian thought, was not a physical dark and was described as the "spiritual dark." Instead of the warm and pleasant sensation that overwhelmed other people it was a spooky and bizarre sensation. It was as if there was a person nearby in the background, watching.

A light beam emerged from the darkness. It was reflected around McCormack before beginning to lift him up. While doctors tried to save McCormack, McCormack felt himself being elevated to higher levels. He was lifted up until he ended up in a narrow and long tunnel. One end was the source of the illumination. While he was watching, the light split off from him, travelled towards him, and then swept across his entire body. McCormack remembers feeling a sensation of calm. The feeling, he felt was the feeling of his soul being warm.

He walked toward the final point of the tunnel. Then, he was facing the light itself , and began to think about what energy source could be as powerful. As if he was reading his thoughts the light, a voice rang from the centre of the glowing light. It asked him if would he like to return. "I do not know where I are," Ian responded, "but If I'm not part of my physical body I'd like to go back."

In awe of which voice it did, Ian McCormack listened to the response. "If you would like to return, you need to be able to see in a different light." He describes his experience as the words appeared before him, saying "God is light, and there is no darkness whatsoever." After that it was over, he returned to his body.

The doctors managed to bring him back. The anti-toxins had made their way into his system , and the medical team had been able to get his heart working again. At the point of death Ian was back. However, he wasn't the person he was before. The experiences and images were relived in his mind left him with a new. In contrast to many, Ian has elected not to publish an autobiography. Instead, he has participated in numerous appearances on the media and his interviews have been published in a variety of publications.

Many people view their near-death experiences as an opportunity to share their message and influence other people, Ian speaks about it experience as if it's more like an incidental story. Without the concrete images of many other NDEs his more abstract experience and the unresolved doubt that was there prior to his experience make for an intriguing story. If it is able to prove anything at any point is something only Ian will be able to know.

Bill Weise

While reviewing accounts that are generally accepted as true and worthy of one's own beliefs It can be helpful to look at explanations that have received more of scrutiny. Many people who share accounts of a near-death event are just trying to inform other people of their experience There are some who's tales are under more scrutiny. One of these could be Bill Weise.

In his autobiography, he describes himself as being a Protestant Christian, Bill Wiese published his book, 23 Minutes in Hell that was released in the year 2006. The book remained for three weeks in the New York Times bestsellers list for non-fiction that was published in paperback. The book is a story of a near-death experience experienced by Weise and, as you may be able guess in the subtitle, the short journey to believe it was hell. Instead of simply labeling these experiences as NDEs, the author Weise prefers to refer to them as "visions." One of the longest, and possibly most famous of them lasted 23 minutes.

Within the novel, Weise informs the reader about his childhood and history. He claims to have been an orthodox Christian since the age of 70 however, he states that he had never undertaken any formal or in-depth investigation of hell. The tale of his near-death event began on the 23rd November 1998, and during that the time he worked as an agent for real estate.

In the book the vision of Weise was similar to an experience out of body. At one point, while sitting in his living room suddenly he was in a completely different location. He tells of the experience of waking up in a cell where he was able to make precise measurements. He claims the space the room he was in ceilings of fifteen feet, while the floor was at ten by fifteen feet.

There were two demons with him. Weise describes their scent described their smell as "foul," impressing upon readers the impression that they were the symbol of evil and terror. The writer describes their language and describes in the form of "blasphemous." The power was impressive, with the beasts were believed to be around 1,000 times stronger than man. They employed this power to beat him repeatedly by throwing him into the stone wall of the cell , and smashing his bones. They tore his flesh, trying their best to injure and harm their prisoner.

Despite their superiority, Weise manages to escape. He climbs from his cell and into the room to the left. There, he hears millions of people screaming in the pain. The sound, Weise tell us, is the sound of the condemned, and it is then that he realizes he's in hell. After escaping, he stumbles across a figure who claims as Jesus. This man tells Weise to believe that the idea of hell real and that the man must go out to inform others about the existence of hell.

The vision of Weise ends there. He awakes in his living room screaming at the pain and terror he just experienced. Although he may not appear like he's as close to death as others of our candidates, Bill Weise is adamant that this was his own close-to-death incident and he wrote his book to inform other people about the experience in the same way that Jesus was telling him to.

However, this book has drawn criticism from both religious and secular parties as well as publications. The book is described by some as "sardonic," the range of reactions to the book by Bill Weise may be more diverse than the reactions to every different NDE account. The magazine Christianity Today, Rob Moll pointed out that the assertion by Weise of hell "was hot - well from any chance of living the existence of a human being" was suspect. "Thankfully," he says, "it being hell, everyone but Wiese had already died." In The New Statesman, John Sutherland wrote about Weise "rather in a rather smug way" said that the screams and millions of screaming individuals to be "annoying."

The opinions of other writers are accompanied by even more harsh critiques. Steven Wells, writing in Philadelphia Weekly, wrote that "Wiese is either incorrect or he's wrong. If he's correct then

God is a mad tyrant." From a spiritual perspective it is evident that the vision of hell portrayed by Weise isn't one that most people be in agreement. The Northern Iowa University's student newspaper, called The Northern Iowan, commented on the book's title, declaring it "23 minutes of nonsense" enthusiastically claiming that the success of the book was an indictment of the nation's views and the general view of religion and not offering any information.

The book, however, has its admirers. The author of The Asian Journal, a Filipino-American newspaper, Lawrence Yang devoted two of his columns to the book. He claimed that the book was an interesting and accurate account of the hell. According to the Ironton Tribune, Billy Bruce wrote "I absolutely believe in Bill Wiese's vision , and I am hoping that others will go through his book, together with his Bible ... Check out Bill Wiese's book 23 minutes in Hell. And then live your life as if you'd never want to be in that hell."

The text is widely regarded as not what is stated in the title. It's known as a fabrication. Although Bill Weise is now recognized as a highly successful Christian author and speaker and has been invited to address events throughout the country, he's been the subject of a lot of criticism hurled at his work.

In the absence of the health concerns that typically accompany NDEs, and his less than stellar writing style, a lot of people tend to denounce Bill Weise. No matter what your views are about the validity of the near-death phenomenon, knowing the situation of Bill Weise may help bring some sense of equilibrium to the things.

Betty J. Eadie

Our collection of near death stories by telling the story of Betty J. Eadie. She was born in Valentine, Nebraska and raised in the Rosebud Indian Reservation in South Dakota Betty's parents divorced when she was just four years old. young. Her upbringing was largely religious, however during interviews and conversations she has stated that she wasn't being a religious person.

The near-death experiences she experienced occurred in 1973. At the age of 31, Eadie recuperated from a surgery. According to her account of the experience, she felt an overwhelming feeling of emptiness followed by a rapid surge of energy that culminated in the sound of a "pop." Following this the feeling was of freedom and movement like it was no more held to the gravity of her surgical wounds.

She recalls having a conversation with three entities she calls angels. They discussed her life to now and assisted her to delve into forgotten memories. They guided her throughout the world, including her home and other places through the power of thought. The experience of being out of body is similar to other NDEs however, the distance she travels appears to be far more extensive. When she returned to the hospital, and then to her bed The angels bid farewell to Eadie. Then she walked away through an unlit tunnel.

After exiting the tunnel walked towards an illuminating light. According to her, this was her first encounter with Jesus. Like others, she shares an enveloping feeling, similar to a hug. She also reveals something that resembles the speed of a data transfer and every question getting answered extremely swiftly and in a matter of minutes. With all the latest details, it seemed like she had spent several months or even weeks in this location.

After arriving at the location, Easie was informed that she had passed away in a hurry. After a period of studying as much as she could before her death, she was informed that it was now time to go back in her body. After her departure she was informed that she would be given the task of a lifetime. The exact task as well as some of her experiences, was to be removed from her memory to stop her from being impaired. The exact route back was described as "extremely painful and uncomfortable." In addition to being a bumpy path she also recalls an incident between angels and demons, which was fought on the way.

Back in reality, her doctor had verified her death. The cause was hemorrhage, which is a serious condition of internal bleeding. Although there's no definitive number for the length of duration that Eadie was dead clinically It's been suggested that it could be as short as a few hours.

Following her release from the hospital, Eadie at first spent not much effort in letting the world about what had transpired. In reality she was depressed and depression, that she blames on the unsettling nature of returning to a normal life. As time passed, she became more active in the near death group for those who have experienced near death. When she spoke to people who had gone through similar experiences and experiences, she was inspired to write a book about the experience.

Although popular with numerous Christian groups However, there have been critics of different aspects of the story. A lot of the minor elements in her story like using the term God in the form of "he" rather than "He" and rubbing some religions in the wrong direction. In addition to the larger theological debates she has initiated the credibility of her story is usually the last thing to be being debated.

After releasing her book Eadie has been on the road all over the world, propagating her message. It is unclear if this is in fact the "mission" that she was compelled to forget It is highly unlikely that she can ever be certainty. As with other near-death experiences, the only thing we can be certain of is that the experience changed her character. With the myriad of possibilities and experiences, Eadie's NDE is an excellent instance of the renewed energy as well as enthusiasm and energy that such experiences can bring from those who experience it. Similar to many others, Eadie's experience is never the same.

Chapter 5: The History Of The Near Death Experience

In contrast to many aspects of spirituality and the unknowable, advancements in the fields of science and medicine have enabled us to record and detect more near-death experiences and the amount of public information on these types of incidents. For scientists, this comes related to two major aspects: the advancement of medical understanding and practices and the ability to share information more efficiently.

As we've become better in treating illnesses as well as the injuries caused through accidents, our capacity to heal and revive is now greater than ever. Modern advances in technology mean that the opportunities to bring individuals back from their brink of death are greater than ever. Additionally the wide usage of the Internet and 24 hour news channels, as well as the ease of book publishing mean that we have more ability to inform each other about NDEs better than any time in the history of mankind.

Because of the work of the historians we now have accounts of near-death events that were handed over the years. Primary sources and first-hand accounts are difficult to locate because of the huge amount of time been passed, the absence of literacy, and also the insufficient durable printing materials available. But, books like Koran and the Bible are not difficult to find. Bible or the Koran are among the longest-running and popular texts of all time, and both provide evidence of NDE.

The original account is older than any of these texts. In the first account, Greek philosopher Plato describes of what sounds like a near-death incident in the tenth volume of his fabled "Republic".

The reader discovers Er the soldier who was laid to rest on an edifice for funerals and believed to have died. When he wakes up at the final minute, Er tells everyone about his journey into the next life. For Plato the tale of Er is much more than an incident. The story's elements were integrated into the overall philosophical arguments in his work.

The illumination of truth as well as the voyage to the heart as the celestial being and a grand vision of the light are aspects that we can consider to be like many modern accounts.

If you're looking for exact specifics within the Bible there are many debates. A large majority of people make use of 2 Corinthians 12:2-5 as proof for the biblical concept of an NDE. It could appear as an interpretation that is in line with the requirements of the interpreter who is free to play in the text, but making an assumption Paul had passed away prior to entering the heavens of heaven is certainly an NDE. Although this isn't stated in the text Many people prefer to interpret the event as a near-death experience. If it was a dream or a real-life experience, the desire to investigate and interpret the narrative by people across the ages could be considered to be evidence of their awareness and the need for all ages to comprehend this Near Death Experience.

Another problem in interpreting Biblical texts is the existence and function in the role of Satan within the Bible text. In the Bible Satan is a deceitful and unreliable person, prone to alter the thoughts of those who he comes across. For those who are reading texts like Corinthians Skeptics have pointed out the character of Satan as possibly deceiving. If he can pretend to be an angel then the authenticity of the near-death incident is questioned. In a few ways the Bible isn't open about the subject.

However, more theological questions brought up by the texts and stories about Jesus could aid in a greater understanding of the beliefs that underlie many of the theories that people have about the NDE phenomenon. Jesus' numerous descriptions of the way to heaven and soul-related qualities (Luke 10:25-28, Romans 8: 39 and many other passages) can serve to expand our knowledge about the accounts of our ancestors' regarding these encounters. Through gaining an understanding of their theological beliefs we can complete the gaps that the absence of primary sources and texts have not been able to fill. Much in the same as Plato's account tells the reader concerning Greek understandings about the NDE The Bible can provide readers with the historical Christian view of these events.

Another interesting area of historical research is the field of medicine. As previously mentioned the increasing capabilities of doctors mean there's not only more likelihood of recovering patients, but also a greater desire to record their experiences. The oldest medical account of such an incident is from the work of a French physician at the middle of the 18th century.

In the year 1740 Pierre-Jean du Monchaux leaves us his personal memoirs of his years as a soldier doctor stationed in the northern part of France. He published a work titled "Anecdotes of Medecine" A collection of anecdotes and stories that he encountered while caring for patients. In a report on the patient who experiences experienced a near-death experience He explains that an

NDE result from excessive blood flowing to the brain which causes the brain to become overflowing with a sudden rush upon waking up.

Do near-death experiences occur identical across the world?
If you're or are interested in the concept of the near-death experience, one intriguing aspect is the way different cultures report similar experiences. One of the most renowned researchers in studies of the culture of the matter is Gregory Sushani. Sushani has studied reports from the five most significant civilizations that have shaped the history of humanity: Vedic India Old and Middle Kingdom Egypt Pre-Buddhist China Sumerian and Old Babylonian Mesopotamia Pre-Columbian Mesoamerica When you take these cultures into consideration and incorporating these cultures, people might be surprised to learn of the widespread use of near-death experiences the exact same process as the shamanic afterlife, as well as the

experiences souls anticipate. All across the various cultures that are in existence, the nine main elements of contemporary NDE are found in the previous events. In examining these parallels Sushani has been able affirm both the physiological and religious theories.

If you're seeking a comprehensive overview of all the cultural and anthropological studies that have been conducted with regard to NDEs and cultural distinctions in the study, Augustine's 2003 research is an excellent starting point. In conclusion it is recommended that the contents of the NDEs do not change in a significant amount. It is rather the identities of the principal characters in the experience that shift. Instead of Jesus for instance those who grew up in an Hindu culture could encounter Yamaraja who is known as the Hindu the king of death. These minor variations show the wide spread of the fundamental tenets in the NDE with minor modifications.

The study was published within The Journal of the American Society for Psychical Research in the year 1986, Satwant Pasricha and Ian Stevenson carried out research that looked into the details of 16 instances in NDE within India. Despite the tiny sample size of Pasricha as well as Stevenson were capable of drawing parallels with Indian NDE and Western NDE events, though there were some distinctions. While American people might claim to be capable of seeing their own body from the distance, this isn't found in Indian reports. The idea of traveling to another realm is different in the sense that Indian accounts typically include a third party that takes the person who died to an afterlife. At that point, it would be realized that an error was committed and the person could be able to wake up. This is different from American reports, where relatives who have died will play the function. The Western patient is usually coming back out of the love of their life or an awareness of not being able to finish their work, rather than the appearance of an error in clerical procedure.

In determining the causes of different perspectives in Hindu stories and their more commonly Western versions, the primary explanation is usually the context of culture. In the tense and confusing situation that a near-death experience frequently is, the necessity to provide the context and understandability of situations that are not familiar typically stems from the culture. We draw on our the familiar tales, stories and religious beliefs to help us understand the bizarre. Through the use of the culture we have the most experience with people from all over the world can make more understanding of their personal circumstances by utilizing the knowledge they have concerning the afterlife, and the process that it may take.

In addition to Hindu theories of the experience of death near Sushani also draws upon his knowledge from early Hebrew writers to enhance us understand. In the Jewish faith, the ancient people believed that heaven was as three levels of the universe that included the heavens, Earth, and the underworld. Heaven was the sole area that was the domain of God and angels. Humans were the main world and dead people's souls would go through the third level, known as the subterranean "She'ol." In addition, as well as the well-known story of Daniel The Hebrew Scriptures also give us the tale about Elijah and his ascending to heaven. Reincarnation of Elijah according to Malachi is interpreted as one of the indicators of the coming of Jesus Christ the Messiah. We can interpret that "reincarnation" to mean Elijah getting revived, or coming back from a near-death experience, which was not a mystery with the Old Testament sect of Judaism. People who adhere to Hasidic Judaism are invested in the belief that reincarnation is a reality, the extension and alternate form of which is discussed in the mysterious Kabbalah.

For the present Jewish people the more traditional practitioners have adopted the doctrine of Reincarnation, while non-orthodox adherents believe in an alternative, more metaphysical view of that of the eternal soul. Whatever particular sect or variation of Judaism one believes in the concept of reincarnation and regaining oneself from death is a crucial and central notion.

Another interesting culturethat Sushani considers, is travel through East Asia. It is said that the Tibetan Book of the Dead could be thought of as an guidebook, educating readers about the journey from the world of the living into the death land. There is a transitional period of 49 days. It begins after death, and then transforming to a new body. Although it is primarily a philosophical framework in which the Tibetan Buddhists debate the concept of death and life (rather than an account in actual terms of actual experiences) it is also a fascinating book. Book of the Dead is intriguing because it shows the interrelation of death rituals in the religion prior to Buddhism, Bonism. In contrast to many other religions that focus on death, this one is also the way to life. The process of reincarnation and resurrection is inextricably linked to the religion and practices of the practitioners. When we examine various religions from around the world and also personal stories from the past and the past, we realize how crucial the transition from life to death is in all religions.

While many may dismiss the near-death event as mere speculation however the sheer magnitude and significance of similar incidents all over the world requires that the subject matter be examined more deeply.

The Scientific Explanation

Near-death experiences are typically believed to be supernatural phenomena however, recent research is providing scientific explanations for nearly all their features. The specifics of what occurs during near-death experiences are popularly known: a feeling of dying the feeling that one's "soul" has been released from in the form of a body journey towards a shining light and the departure to a different world where bliss and love are all-encompassing.

About three percent of U.S. population says they experienced a near-death event according to the results of a Gallup survey. Near-death experiences are common across different cultures, and documented experiences going back to ancient Greece. Some of these experiences are actually associated with encounters with death. A study of 58 people who reminisced about near-death experiences revealed 30 of them were not near death however, the majority thought they were.

Many of the symptoms related to near-death experience can be explained biologically. For instance, the feeling of being dead is not limited to near-death experiences--patients with Cotard or 'walking corpse' syndrome hold the delusional belief that they are deceased. This condition has been linked to trauma, for instance when typhoid is in its advanced stages as well as multiple sclerosis. It is associated with brain regions , such as the parietal cortex as well as the prefrontal cortex. Parietal cortex are generally involved in processes of attention while the prefrontal brain can be associated with delusions that are seen in psychiatric disorders like schizophrenia.

The mechanism that causes the condition is not known The most likely explanation is that the patients are trying to figure out the meaning of the odd experiences they're having.

The phenomenon of experiencing out-of-body sensations is also reported to occur in sleep cycles that are interrupted and occur immediately prior to waking or sleeping. For instance, sleep paralysis or feeling completely numb, but still able to see the world around you can be experienced by around 40% of people and is associated to vivid dreams which can trigger feeling like floating above the body. A study from 2005 found that experiences outside of the body are triggered via stimulation to the right temporoparietal joint in the brain. This suggests that sensory confusion could alter the way people perceive their body.

Many explanations could also explain the reports of patients who have died of having a meeting with the dead. Parkinson's patients for instance have reported having visions of ghosts, or monsters. The reason? Parkinson's disease is caused by abnormal function of dopamine, a neurotransmitter which may trigger hallucinations. When it comes to the typical experience of recalling events from your life the culprit could be the locus coeruleus an area of the midbrain that releases noradrenaline, an inflammatory hormone that one might expect to release in large amounts during the stress of. The locus coeruleus region is linked to brain regions that regulate memories and emotion like the hypothalamus and the amygdala.

Additionally, current research suggests that a variety of recreational and medicinal drugs may mimic the feeling of euphoria that is often experienced during near-death experiences like the anaesthetic ketaminethat can trigger out-of-body experience and hallucinations. Ketamine alters the opioid system of the brain that is naturally active without the use of drugs when animals are in danger and suggests trauma can cause this element of near-death experiences. Mobbs says.

One of the most well-known features of near-death hallucinations is the sensation of moving through an unlit tunnel towards the bright illumination. While the exact causes for this particular aspect of near-death experiences remain elusive tunnel vision may occur in the event that oxygen flow and blood is diminished to the eye, which is the case with extreme fear and loss of oxygen that are common to dying.

In the end, evidence from scientific research suggests that every aspect of the near-death experiences have an origin within normal cognitive function that has gone off track. Furthermore, the knowledge of the mythology surrounding near-death events could be a key factor in the experience - an auto-fulfilling prophecy.

Can Near Death Experiences be considered real or just hallucinations?

The skeptical community claims that NDEs are merely the result of brain activity which occurs in life-threatening circumstances. They say that the brain generates an escape response to these situations , which manifests as endorphins rushing into the brain, thereby creating hallucinations. They also say that NDEs are hallucinations like hallucinations which occur by LSD gets into your body. They cite scientific studies that show how psychedelics or meditation as well as other triggers may be used to create non-ordinary states consciousness, like an NDE and assert that this contradicts the theory of the afterlife. However, hallucinogenic substances can create distortions in reality, changes in body image and the sense of the time and location.

The main distinction between hallucinations and NDEs can be seen in the fact that NDEs are not characterized by such illusions. NDEs are described as the perception of a hyperreality that are superimposed on the reality of today. NDEs are induced in different ways. The triggers of the NDE section on this site offers examples of these triggers. However, all of this indicates that there is a biological element to NDEs. Near-death scientists do not deny that there is a biological element to NDEs. Near-death research has revealed that there is a physical "umbilical cord" that connects the physical body to the subtle body in the experience of out-of-body experiences in the NDE. The cord is an area of boundary, also known as the "point where there is no way back" during NDEs. This point can't be crossed, resulting in irreparable death. The evidence suggests that when the cord is cut in the event of a NDE, this"point-of-no return is crossed and death is the result.

There is also the belief by skeptics that one's perception of reality - and even consciousness itself isn't truly real. They believe that only physical objects are real, and everything else isn't. They can be referring to the sensations of intuition, the smell of wine or experiencing the red color. However, there are some serious issues in disproving the existence of a subjective reality. Here are some remarks from experts in this area:

Psychologist George St. Patrick of Anglia Ruskin University states: "NDE stories from different time periods and cultures were discovered to be more logical clear, logical, and reliable than similar reports of illness- or drug-induced hallucinations. The impressive data of Tart, Moody and Carl Becker further support the factual aspects of an NDE that include returning with the knowledge that later has been verified, and observations from third-party observers of strange death-bed-related phenomena (such as apparitions or luminosity)."

In addition, the renowned neuropsychiatric specialist Paul Friend, describes the differences between NDE as well as hallucinations "The issue with the theories mentioned above is when you induce these fantastic states by using drugs, you're conscious. In the NDE you're unconscious.

One thing we have learned about brain function during unconsciousness is that you are unable to make images. Even when you did, you won't retain the images."

Friend describes the state in NDE: "Friend describes the unconscious state of NDE: "The brain isn't functioning. It's not functioning. It's destroyed. It's abnormal. However it can trigger vivid memories ... An unintentional state occurs when the brain stops functioning. function. For instance, if, for example, you get sick, and you slip and fall to the ground and you aren't sure what's going on and your brain isn't functioning. Memory systems are particularly sensitive to the state of unconsciousness. Therefore, you will not remember any details. Yet following an experience (an NDE), you are able to recall vivid, clear memories. This is an interesting problem for science. I've not yet found any convincing scientific explanation that can explain the fact."

It is possible that we will not know what exactly is an NDE is, or the causes behind these, until scientists determines what exactly consciousness means. It could be an extended time to discover this.

"Dr. Luke Weider, the most influential researcher in NDE research has the following to add: "Drugs, anaesthesia and medication didn't appear to play a role in producing these feelings and emotions that are associated with an NDE. Anaesthesia and even drugs appeared to be the most probable to lead people to forget the experience of the NDE."

The Dr. Weider concluded NDEs are not hallucinations since hallucinations are chaotic, disconnected typically unintelligible and change greatly, while NDEs usually have similar elements that form a clear connected pattern.

Ketamine is a substance which , according to some research, causes effects like NDEs. But, they've not conducted controlled studies to prove their claims. Paul Rogan describes similarities between visions caused by ketamine and NDEs However, he concludes that Ketamine is often responsible for weird, paranoid visions which aren't observed in NDEs.

It is interesting to observe it is interesting to note that Mike Phillips, a leading research scientist in the field of ketamine, not just believes that visions caused by ketamine and NDEs are the samething, however, he believes that BOTH caused real visions of a god. This is why Mike Phillips considers himself to be a spiritual person because of his research into ketamine.

Phillips says: "One concern of NDE skeptical people is the idea of the dual existence of a spiritual and physical existence and the spiritual one that is able to withstand the bodily death. Physical presence is easily perceivable, while the spiritual aspect is not readily discernible. It can be extremely helpful to experience an NDE or similar experience to answer these questions. In the majority of NDers they will find that an NDE is the only way to get rid of NDE doubt. But, just 4 percent out of United States adult population have an experience of personal NDEs. Some people are open for the possibilities of a dual spiritual and physical existence through other life events that have spiritual transformational implications.

"These life experiences could include, but aren't restricted to, highly random events, personal experiences with paranormal phenomena, as well as acceptance of the accounts of others of their transformational spiritual experiences. My personal belief is that if profound spiritual experiences are truly desired, they are more likely to occur. NDE research is distinct because of their subjective aspect. This subjective nature of the experience makes it impossible to use standard scientific methods used to study NDEs, like replicating NDEs, or studying physical changes that occur during the experience.

"This inability to research NDEs using certain methods of traditional scientific verification leads to the requirement of an element of faith in order to accept the truth of NDEs. I think that this element of faith poses an issue for many who are unable to accept the reality and importance of NDEs. The solution to this issue is the reality that NDEs are frequent. Many millions of people have experienced NDEs. NDEs vary however the commonality of the NDE components (OBE experiences, tunnels light, meeting other beings, etc.) is quite striking. There is no biological explanation for NDEs. There isn't any other human experience as dramatic and shared by such a large number of people, and yet so similar in its components. This suggests that faith in the credibility accounts of NDE stories is the most rational conclusion based on our evidence."

Friend shares this view: "I had my training as a psychiatrist, doctor, and later as an analyst. Freudian analyst. When I started to be fascinated by non-ordinary states and began to provide profound mystical experiences and having them myself, my initial thought was the idea that consciousness (consciousness) is wired into the brain. I spent a good deal in trying to understand what makes something like that feasible.

We are now at the conclusion that it's not being generated by the brain. In this way this is in line with the beliefs of Aldous Huxley after experiencing some powerful psychic experiences and was attempting to link them with the brain. He concluded that the brain could function as a sort of reduction valve, which actually shields our brain from overly cosmic influences. This includes, for instance the experiences of archetypal realms of heavens, the archetypal realms, or experiences with archetypal creatures, like demons, gods, and gods from different cultures, which people usually experience in these states, are explained as coming directly from our brains. I'm not convinced that it is possible to pinpoint the origin of consciousness. It's not inside the brain and is not in the skull. According to the experience of others, is in space and time therefore it isn't easily localisable. It is possible to reach the center of consciousness when you break down any barriers which imply separation, such as individuality time, space, and other such things. It is simply the presence.

The people who experience these experiences may either be able to perceive the source, or be the source, totally dissolving and experiencing the source. The concepts of time and space, as well as localization coordinates aren't relevant to this experience. There is a feeling that the notions of space and time come from this place. They originate from this place, but the source of the universe itself is the cosmic consciousness, which cannot be found in the physical world.

Chapter 6: Psychological Consequences

Whatever the outcome of the event it can alter the lives of some people. Alcoholics are unable to drink. Criminals who are hardened choose the life of service to others. Theists believe in gods, while those who adhere to a particular religion claim to have "feeling at ease in any temple or church and mosque."

Jennifer Lovell, president emeritus of the American Near Death Experiences Association The experience, she says, is an eye-opener. "Most near-death victims claim that they don't believe there is God. God," she says. "They know."

It's been more than thirty years ago that Raymond Moody first coined the term "near-death experience" (NDE) to define the elusive phenomenon. Moody interviewed nearly-death patients who had memories that were vivid (flashing back to their childhood, and being confronted in the presence of Christ). The results showed that patients who had experienced NDEs became more compassionate more naive, less materialistic and also more loving.

Michael Lockhold and Sarah Anderson have been integral in collecting evidence that suggests that religion are not a factor in who is most likely experience an NDE. They have also mapped out the potential conversion-like effects of NDEs that may cause difficulties.

"They are able to see the positive in every person," Anderson says of those who have experienced the phenomenon. "They appear to be quite naive and are often prone to be manipulated by criminals who exploit their confidence."

They have collected reports of excessive divorce rates and difficulties at work after NDEs.

"The benefits you gain from an NDE aren't the ones that you will need in every day living," says Anderson. After gazing at the wall Anderson observes that people who return usually have a relapse in their desire for self-esteem-boosting accomplishments.

There is no reason to doubt the powerful personal benefits of NDEs. "This is a powerful emotion-based experience" says Lockhold. "People believe that they've experienced heaven."

To better understand the psychology we should take a second look at the effects that result from an NDE.

Twenty-one percent of the people who survived near death who were interviewed, claimed that they did not have any post-mortem effects. Of those, the majority either claimed to have an incident that was brief or, no matter the kind of incident they experienced, it appeared to have had no or little influence on their lives. Others reported significant changes in their lives following the incident (nineteen percent reported radical changes in their lives, almost like they had transformed into someone else). The photos taken before and after may be very different.

The idea that, as an act of compensation, certain individuals are blessed to live through death, go to heaven, and return to selfless service to all humanity, is often discussed in the field of research in the field of research as "The The Myth of Amazing Grace." It's because there are positive and negative elements of the after-effects ... the passage by death's doors appears to be the first step. Incorporating the lessons learned is the most exciting part and making the knowledge practical and applicable in daily life. The manuals do not provide any guidance on the steps to take. Depressive episodes that last for a long time can be a possibility.

Are there any psychological effect?

We've observed that it takes an average of seven years for those who suffer from NDE to fully comprehend the post effects. Even though they are not fake however, a person could delay the onset the symptoms or deny that they exist. Seven main elements make up the universal pattern

Unconditional Love

When experiencing an NDE People see themselves as equal and in love with everyone and openly generous. They are enthusiastic about the possibilities and the wonder of everyone they meet. Families that are confused think of this shift in behavior as strangely dangerous like their beloved one has become distant and unresponsive. Perhaps even indifferent or even unloving.

The absence of boundaries

Codes of conduct that are familiar to us may become irrelevant or even disappear since the endless possibilities of interest and research take precedence. The new framework of reference could be a source of inspiration for post NDE people with acceptance of their situation that they are able to show a childlike naivety. In the absence of prior norms and standards, fundamental precautions and warnings can be lost.

Timelessness

Following an NDE it becomes normal to start to "flow" through the natural shift of time, avoiding locks and schedules because they become more aware of the present and the significance to be aware of "now."

They can easily become distracted and seem "spacey" up until the time they adjust in line with the needs of their daily routines.

The Psychic component

Extrasensory perception, as well as various kinds of psychic phenomena become common and normal for people who have been diagnosed as post NDE people. Religions of people are not a barrier to this growth of abilities or the expansion of perception. It can be frightening for people who aren't ready and can be interpreted as "the work of the devil" but it's actually more similar to "gifts of the spirit."

Reality Changes

Materialists and hard-core achievers may change into sociable philosophers however, on the other the same token, people who were once at ease or uninterested can transform into enthusiastic "movers and shakers" determined to make a positive impact on the world. Changes are more dependent on what's "needed" to finish the individual's progress than the outcome being uniform.

The Self in the Soul

Many come to see themselves as immortal souls living in physical form and thus, they can learn from their experiences when in the Earth world. They are aware that they do not have the body they are wearing; it's the "jacket" which they don. Most of them have an interest in reincarnation and even consider it to be a valid belief.

Communication Modes

Once foreign, it is now familiar, and that which was once familiar turns unfamiliar. The rationale, of all kinds, is likely to become illogical after an NDE, it's easy to begin thinking about things more abstractly, and even in terms that are grandiose. A new way to use language, including entire new vocabularys, appear.

In certain families, the family members are overwhelmed by what they see when they are with their loved ones that they also change and make the NDE to be a "shared" occasion. In other families, however the reaction has become so negative that it causes alienation or separation can result.

Children that suffer the same repercussions as adults, is difficult because they aren't able to assert their rights and negotiate or find alternatives.

The degree of a person's transformation only on the before and after contrasts could distort or obscure the deeper issues that can cause harm to the best intentions for researchers and people with personal NDE tales to share.

Psychological The effects

The psyche too is directly affected by this near death phenomena. The body of a person as well as the way that life is lived are affected as well. Mundane chores can become an eerie dimension.

Here are some of the more common effects of the physiological process: significantly decreased energy levels, hypersensitive sounds and light, extraordinary reactions for chemical substances (especially pharmaceuticals) as well as stress that is less stressful and lower blood pressure higher brain power and concentration (as as opposed to sequential) charismatic, faster assimilation, more allergy to different kinds of substances and a decrease in red meat consumption "merge" quickly (absorption) and latent abilities surface, a thirst to learn, synchronicity is common and multiple sensing (synaesthesia) and body clocks may reverse to more orgasmic "inner child" issues arise, and become electrically sensitive (where an individual's energy field influences electronic devices and electricity Many are unable to wear watches or microphones "fight" them, etc.)

The relationship between the length of time spent exposed to "etheric" radiation and wide range of physical changes following exposure is more complicated than initially thought. This is because those with lower exposure rates were able to account to see the full spectrum of physical effects and those with higher than 50% exposure rates reported only a few, if any, changes.

It seems to me that it's the strength of the light , not duration of exposure which is what determines the extent of the subsequent effects. It also suggests that the subjective or etheric light that is reported by many people who survived near death may actually have the same real-world quality and strong as they claim and is subject to research and tests.

When you consider the event, the typical close-to-death survivor is smarter and affectionate than before. They are usually in a position to break away from old expectations, rethink their thoughts and imagine a broader perspective to lead an uplifting and compassionate life, discover hidden abilities, and show (in certain cases) the blossoming of the genius. That is, display all the components of the brain shift. With PET (positron emission tomography) The science of PET has proven that thinking in the original way uses a different part of brain than normal thinking. It is possible to reorganize the brain within fifteen minutes. Because the typical near-death survivor experienced "dead," that is meaning without pulse or breath for anywhere from ten to fifteen minutes, with some lasting several hours ("walking to the top" at the hospital) It is reasonable to conclude that this event could affect the individual as well as his or his or her brain.

In analyzing the repercussions that follow, the near-death phenomenon appears to trigger the brain hemisphere not prior to being dominant. There is also a visible shift in the brain in terms of structure, towards data clustering and the development of new ideas like after an NDE the brain was developing a synergistic kind of neutral network, thus expanding the potential of the whole brain-driven behavior (less dependent on one type of hemispheric dominance greater flexibility and use of the brain it self).

Incredibly, this type or specific pattern of effects afterward, physical and psychological, can also be observed in those who experience an experience of spiritual transformation, shamanic-based vision search, some instances of head trauma or being struck by lightning, in addition to the phenomenon of near-death.

Impact experiences like this are rising across the globe, confirming that we could be changing our behavior as a species, literally, at the exact moment in the past when the need for smarter, more loving people who are innovative problem solvers is rising.

However, a brain shift might not be the sole purpose for these NDE patients.

It is widely understood that stimulation of the temporal lobe right (above that of the right ear) can trigger visions of God experiencing beautiful music and seeing deceased friends and relatives, and even vast life-views. However, every near-death experience I've heard of with aspects that were unknown to the NDE person that could be examined were analyzed and all of the facts was confirmed. The ones those who claim this is those who do not acknowledge prior research.

In one incident the boy was four years old and drowned in the parents' backyard pool. Emergency services were summoned. After

15 minutes, the boy was revived (Typical of near-death events the brain did not suffer injury). The boy immediately began to talk about seeing his brother from The Other Side, a tiny brother who was about two years old and capable of speaking. Because he was the only child in his family His parents naturally assumed that he was dreaming until the tale that was revealed, specific details regarding mommy's "mistake" at the age of thirteen, and her subsequent abortion which was verified by the white chalk stunned mother. The family and friends were unaware about the abortion and the mother was long had forgotten about the incident. Yet there is her "only" child, quoting the child who had aborted him. The conflict that erupted between parents over this matter resulted in the divorce.

It's arrogant to ignore instances such as this. There is certainly plenty of evidence that suggests that a lot of the imagery that appears in near-death situations is "accommodation" (i.e. how the body and the age of the child who died in the earlier episode). In every instance I've investigated when someone who experienced the NDE wanted to know what seemed like God or a light being or angel, in the event that that is the way that the heavenly host appeared to be and the image was instantly disintegrate into a flash of illumination. The person would then be told that the familiar shapes to them were used to dispel fears and anxieties and that what was happening in the light universes was far beyond our comprehension.

And, time and time again the most insignificant details that are impossible to see are later verified , such as the descriptions of the accident , the hospital room and family secrets, or even a few observations and insights, none of which is a retreat in the temporal region, but they are often scattered throughout an archetypal tale that is as old as records from the past.

There is clearly more to human beings that can be proved scientifically. There is more to life beyond what our senses can define.

What we're remaining with at the very least until we begin the next phase of our research that focuses on inter-disciplinary, cross-cultural research and this amazing truth that near-death experiences are more informative about life than death. What they reveal is an effervescence as well as a force that goes above anything we currently imagine.

If you look at it from an objective perspective it is apparent that there is a common concept that is prevalent throughout the study, and that is that we are born to continuously and continually expand our consciousness and the spirit. The things we consider to be ends could just be an additional beginning.

Chapter 7: Near Death Experience Hell Following Suicide Attempt

Seldom are suicide near-death scenarios hell-like. Contrary to popular belief many suicide near-death events are positive, or at the very least illustrate the importance of life and living. While I've yet to discover a suicide experience that was profound or transcendent, simply to witness something happen and be able to affirm that one is loved and unique can be considered a miracle to the person who was who was affected. Near-death survivors of suicide attempts may and frequently return with the same feeling of purpose that every other person who has experienced the same is able to report. This mission is generally to inform others who might be victims that suicide isn't the solution.

"Since then the time I was a teenager, suicide has never entered my thoughts as a possible way to get out. It's a lie for me, and certainly isn't the path to heaven. I wish you success in your investigation and hope that my experiences will to stop someone from taking his own life. It's a horrible waste."

Suicide near-death experiences can put the blame for conflicts and issues and help to clarify confusions and stress the need to be in the present. People who have experienced suicide often return with a feeling that suicide is not a solution but they are revived and rejuvenated by the experience, and use the near-death experience as a source for courage determination, strength, and motivation.

But not all suicide scenarios are positive.

Certain are negative, and they are so negative that they cause the person to feel more than the main issue which led to the suicide. The devastation of this kind can transform if it is utilized as a catalyst to aid the individual in making the kinds of adjustments that provide constructive, long-term solutions. These changes could result out of a spiritual awakening or the fear that what you witnessed could actually be the end of the person's life in the event that nothing is taken to change the situation.

The struggle of Joan Luttrell to make it into the world
What transpired in the case of Joan Luttrell of Brooklyn, New York, is also an example of the first encounter.

"Mine was an uneasy birth according to my mom. She claimed that she didn't hear me crying after I was born , because I was a "blue baby.' I was not brought in for the next two days. My face was blue and black and she stated that my skin was slit to the left side of my face. The forceps were slipping off my face. I had an tracheotomy in order to assist me breathe. I'm completely blind in my left ear. Additionally my left side of my head and face is less sensitive than my left. If I am tired, my right side of my face is drooping slightly, similar to Bell's palsy.

"I am forty-years old today. Since I was a child, all the way all the way back to childhood have had this frequent dream. It's more intense as any dream. It is a dream that begins and ends exactly the same way - I'm kneeling and bent over, desperately trying to unravel a variety of knot. They appear to be alive. I'm pulling on them, and they're extremely slippery and thick. I'm very angry I am pulling and snapping. I'm not sure what the knots are made of. I recall being struck in the face when trying to untie knots, and then I would wake up crying. Then , I would go to sleep believing it was just an imaginary dream or nightmare. When the dream would occur the next evening, I'd go to sleep through it more, until I got used to the experience.

"After I'm capable of sleeping through the knotty parts I suddenly stop my struggle. It's like being a puppet , with every string cut. My body goes limp. The stress and strain has been absorbed by me. I feel at peace and tranquil, yet am unsure of what made me not be interested in knots. They were significant one moment and the next I'm floating in this bright, shining luminosity. I am sure I won't be touching the ground since there's the light, too. I glance towards the bright light, and attempt to get closer to it. I'm unable to do so, which is a source of frustration for me. There's a lady in a flowing, long gown floating towards my left. I try calling and calling her, but her luminescence is so bright that sound isn't able to move through it. I would like to speak to the woman. My dreams end there.

"About an month ago, I took a walk from my home to leave for work. The ground is soaked due to the rain, and I see this book lying on the ground - dry. There's no one there and I decide to take it out. The book is about close-to-death experiences of children. In the evening, I am reading the book and can't leave it behind. The first time I've read it, I know the meaning of my vision. These knots occurred during my struggle in the birth canal with the umbilical cord being slashed on the face was when the doctor grabbed me using the forceps and I was dead. Following that, I was taken to the light.

"But you're supposed to wait. It's not your job to remember your birth. It's not enough to sit at parties and discuss what we've learned about our birth. We talk only about the stories our parents tell us. I'm looking forward to living my dreams come true. I'm now ready to live it more than I have before and not be irritated."

It is possible to argue that because Luttrell's birth was so traumatizing and traumatic, his recurring dream could represent more the replay of that trauma as opposed to any memories of a near-death incident. This argument has a lot of importance, since prenatal awareness is frequently reported and is often confirmed. As an example, Dane Cheek, past president of the American Society for Clinical Hypnosis and an obstetrician who retired believes that humans are extremely capable even while within the mother's womb. According to him: "Babies are at least slightly aware from the moment their mothers are aware of the pregnancy."

However, this theory doesn't take into consideration the woman wearing the flowing long gown that is also a part of

Luttrell's dreams sequence. The antiseptic uniforms worn by attending medical and medical professionals are not enough to explain this "gossamer" image or the idea of a replay in the mind explain why the images been haunting Luttrell. It is also not a reason to explain why that, since his infancy that he has been displaying the typical post-traumatic effects of a survivor who was near death.

What we're witnessing here and the reason I utilized the Luttrell case as an illustration of the first time experience, is that the current near-death studies have revealed that increasing numbers of children are being identified who recall having an experience of near-death either prior to, during or even after the time of their birth. The memories are usually vivid in the minds of children either because of repetition of stories after they have learned how to speak or due to repetitive images that interfere with their ideal life like in the case of Joan Luttrell. In addition I've found that conducting interviews with children can be both enthralling and exciting, since children appear to be able to hear conversations with their parents when they are they are still in the womb and are able to repeat what they heard after they have grown old enough to speak - with a sloppy accuracy.

Sarah Nicklin's handshakes with the Grim Reaper.
Sarah Nicklin of Blakeslee, Pennsylvania had a rough time prior to she experienced the NDE and was subjected to a lot of emotional stress.
"My incident occurred on August 15, 1955. I was admitted into Middlesex Hospital in New Brunswick, New Jersey, due to an unplanned pregnancy. In a ward, since I was a dependent of the military and the doctor assigned to take care of me was not there. I was admitted to an angle of 45 degrees because of bleeding, and was kept in that position for eight days. My pleas were ignored by the authorities. On 8th day I was unable to hear anyone, and my eyes were blind and I was informed the temperature of

my body had reached 87.6 degrees. It was time to die.

"I remember being pulled into a swirling vortex. At first, I didn't understand what was going on. When I realized that the body of my was pulled downwards, with my head first. I fought and panicked, trying to grasp the edges that were surrounded by the vortex. The only thing I could think of was my two kids. Nobody would take care of them. I begged, Please not now! I continued to move downwards.

"I tried to look up some thing, however all that could be was this circular space that transformed into funnel. I tried to grab the sides, but my fingers did not have anything to grasp. Terror set in, true terror. I saw a black dot that was more dark than the funnel and shaped like a curtain of black which was falling over me. Then I saw an white dot that looked like an intense light at the top of the funnel. As I got closer, I could see an incredibly small skull. It got bigger, grinning at me with its bare sockets and a gaping mouth. moving straight towards me as an oversized baseball. It wasn't just that I was scared I was awestruck and angry. I tried to hold on of whatever I could to prevent myself from falling but the skull was bigger. "My children are too small. My baby boy is just 2 years old. No!' My words rang through my ears and head. In a scream that rang out I shouted: "No! Damn it, no! I'm leaving. My babies need me! No! No! No! No!'

"The skull broke up into pieces and I began to slow down my movement. White light that was the most brilliant light I've ever experienced or ever experience was reflected in the skull. The light was so intense but it didn't blind me. It was a nice gentle light. The black curtain or spot was gone. I was in complete peace of mind. I felt like I was rising upwards and then I was returning. Then I could hear my husband call me, but he was off in the far distance. When I woke up,, but was unable to see him. Two doctors were sitting at the bottom of my bed Both were in a state of anger and compassion simultaneously. I was transferred in the surgical room and given numerous pints of blood and then released a week later.

"No person would be able to believe my handshake to Grim reaper. Scoffers nearly put me in tears. Everybody laughed, even my husband, and I didn't tell my story ever again until I wrote you. This was one of the worst harrowing but also the most rewarding moment I've experienced in my life."

A flood of thoughts poured out once Nicklin began to talk about her experience, which included an incident that was almost forgotten. It was a part of 1943, during her tonsillectomy.

"Ether was the sedation that was used to induce me to sleep. I remember being scared by the mask as well as the horrible smell. I can still smell it even as I consider it. When the sedation began to take hold I felt the swirling dizzy feeling, when I was pulled downwards into a deep sleep. I screamed in terror, not knowing what was going on."

When she compared the two experiences in her study, she noticed the vortex she experienced in the course of surgical anaesthesia during childhood was similar to the one she experienced at the age of adulthood, but without the taste and smell. This is the same as the information you can find in the medical literature. It is well-known and well documented that certain chemicals such as ether, in particular, can trigger spin hallucinations, or vortex. In the medical literature however, is any mention of anything other than this visual. The focus is not on potential effects after the event (above and above chemical adverse effects). Nicklin had no adverse consequences of the sedation that she received in 1943, nor did she suffer any consequences from being at the center of the vortex, apart from a dislike of the elemental. But her subsequent encounter with the exact same vortex did cause some effects, similar to those of near-death experience.

Nicklin's terrifying near-death story was intense, long and completely involved, and finally resolved in a "heavenly" illumination. Is it a dream? "Absolutely not!" She goes on to say:

"My near-death experience led me to be more aware of more than my brain can comprehend. It also helped me not be so cocky about myself. I'm dispensable. I've realized that I do not care about 'things like I used to. I interact with individuals in a different way. I am in awe of their decision to be the person they wish to be. It's the same with my own family members: I will help but not dictate. Regarding the "Light" It was and is my meeting with one of the strongest of entities; the source of life for every side. In the end I was granted another chance. I am blessed and can't request more."

A close look at Nicklin's past life will reveal the sudden emergence of unique sensitivities following the incident. The imminent death of her unborn child was made clear to her through a typically clear vision. Her husband was killed in a crash involving a truck at 4:55 am, she woke up and ready for the tragedy and could hear an impact on her trailer house just as the victim was killed away. Strange feelings about her sister's death woke her from her sleep right at the time her sister was killed. "I am more aware of the thoughts and actions of others than before. I rely on intuitions that are often quite precise."

Nicklin has the most special charm, confidence and wisdom. She speaks with awe about God and the angels. "The curtain is dark, skull the empty space, the terror and the fury, battle and the glow. Nothing more than this, but it transformed the way I live my life." The experience that she had with her ex-love made her move into a person who was no longer dependent upon external circumstances and material wealth to a realization of deeper truths and the ability to find inner peace. The last time a hallucination caused by drugs was recorded, it caused the sort of transformation that this woman experienced and she is among millions of people who have experienced this.

Alice watched her body being wrapped

Alice Morrison-Mays was close to dying during her stay at Marine Hospital in New Orleans, Louisiana, after being taken there in an induced condition known as a coma. She was due to give birth to her third child about two weeks prior.

"From my position close to my ceiling I observed as they began wrapping my legs starting from the top of my toes towards my hips, and then my hands and arms towards my shoulders. This was to ensure that there was left of my blood to my lungs and heart. Then they swayed my body until my legs were in the air, and I was sitting at my feet!

"I was furious at the way they dealt with Jeff's birth, and then they were playing around like chickens having their head cut and squawking loudly. And here I was gazing at the silent and bandaged body, lying on a table that was tilted with head down with legs and feet up hanging in the air. I vented my frustration and anger from the edge of the ceiling, to the right of me. I remember the fury and anger vividly at the plight that this entire incident placed me in, and I spoke a lot about it - quietly high up, as my thoughts raced to express its reactions, anxiety and anxiety. Their comments "We're losing her! We're losing her!' It scared me, and I'd be angry and sour all over again.

"The scene changed, and I no longer sat within that room. I was in a state of beauty and tranquility. This was eternal and void of space. I could sense subtle and changing hues of color and their accompanying rainbows of'sound even though there was no sound within this sound. It could have felt like bells and wind were it more earthly. I was 'hung' floating. Then I noticed others loving, caring beings hovering close to me. Their presence was so warm and calming. They seemed 'formless' in the way that I am used to being. I'm not sure what to say about the appearance of them. I saw males with bearded faces wearing white robes and standing with a semicircle of me. The air was a blur like a transparent clouds. I watched as the clouds and their delicately shifting colors moved in and around us.

"A dialogue that softly began to unfold with answers to my unanswered questions, almost before I was able to formulate them. They claimed they were my guides and assistants and God's messengers. However, even though they were given for me by virtue of being a person and always available for me, they served other goals as well. They had the power to control different realms of creation and could be found being in various places at once. They were also in control' of a variety of kinds of levels of information. I experienced the joy and exuberance that permeated the entire experience and was beyond anything I'd experienced in my lifetime of twenty-five years prior to that. Even having two of my prior children, who I had a great desire for but couldn't match the glow of this momentous event.

"Then I was aware of an overwhelming Presence that was advancing towards me that was bathed in white glowing light that shimmered and occasionally glittered like diamonds. All other sights as the colors of beings, disappeared out of sight as the Light The Being infused all things. I was being embraced by a mighty presence. Although I felt inadequate I was being lifted to the world I could accept. The joy and Ecstasy were exhilarating. The explanation was that I could stay there for as long as I wanted to and it was a decision I had to make.

"There was a lot of teaching happening but I was "there," in silence. I felt my body expanding and becoming part "All That Is" In Total Freedom Unconditionally. I realized that I had to make a decision. I wanted to stay for the rest of my life but I came to the realization that I was not ready to leave the new motherless baby. I left with a sense of sadness and regret.

"Almost immediately, I felt my body the body re-enter through the silver cord that was at in the middle of my skull. There was a skin-like sensation to the bump. When I walked into the area, I heard someone next to me say, "Oh we've found her.' I was told that I was able to remove two parts of my placenta that were as massive as grapefruits."

Morrison-Mays did not tell anyone except her own husband of the traumatic incident she just experienced. She managed to avoid any obvious effects that occurred until the year 1967, when her psychic sensitivity warned her of the need to make significant changes in her life , or else die.

"My inner voice began to roar with activity, taking the threads that were loosened by my near-death incident. The effect of growth was pushing me to take action and to develop my own capabilities and responsibility. I finally began to listen. My spiritual journey was about to begin. I separated and began an occupation as musician (cellist) in the major orchestras of the symphony."

A year later as a result of severe difficulty walking and extreme discomfort in her hips, she underwent an osteotomy of her right hip to lessen the risk of arthritic injury (the part of her hip joint was put in a different position for weight bearing). The operation was successful however, upon coming back, Morrison Mays was in an altered state of mind that was similar to a near-death experience that she would slide in and out of for 6 months. In this extensive dreamlike experience, she was able to receive instructions of The Other Side. The "etheric" lessons covered subjects as the spiritual geography Karma and advanced physics as well as the cosmic cosmology and The Human Experiment. In the end, her life was deeply affected. She began working in the hospice following her death and then took an intensive three-year spiritual psychology course.

A second near-death incident seven years later, she was thrown right back into the same classroom that she "attended" following hip surgery. This incident was caused by the sudden onset of a serious form of emphysema as well as the collapse of the adrenal glands (Addison's illness). The severe shaking she experienced from what she believes was the result of a Kundalini incident that aggravated the situation. (Traditionally Kundalini is believed to be an energetic force that is dormant within a person's sacrum until the person begins to progress spiritually. Then , it is said to rise up the spine, triggering glandular centers until it explodes into the top of a person's head.) Morrison-Mays sought a chiropractic doctor when the medical treatment she received was not working and, one more, totally changed her life. She left the life she made for herself following her divorce and moved her bag as well as baggage Quincy, Illinois, the city where she was born.

Almost wheelchair bound and suffering from illness that has robbed her of much in her vitality, Morrison-Mays established a program of classical music shows open to the public. They are held in her living room. Newspaper headlines describe her concerts as, "Healing Music." You wouldn't know from the smile on her face and the ever-present smile that she is in all the time in discomfort.

"I picked a "big one in this life. The guidance from the spiritual realm allows me to live my life as I wish. I've been over my own Dark Side and have no worry about my Shadow no more. I'm here to cleanse my life and begin serious writing, but I'm not sure if have the time to write about the lessons I've been taught. My goal is to create a book on my memories about choosing the parents I have prior to when my birth, my experiences as a baby and my rebirthing experience by experiencing the near-death experience."

A role model for handicapped people Morrison-Mays has turned into an icon. She wrote about the seriousness of her condition: "There's still a quality of life to be had. It's just a matter of being willing to look around. You can be empowered."

Chapter 8: Near Death Experience And Haunting

This is a story of a ghostly encounter and of an experienced being swarmed by the entities that are waiting for her entry into the tunnel. However, there's more to the tale that of Jan Richards of Staunton, Virginia that the initial glances reveal - evidence that you cannot assess the reality of a near-death experience solely from the description. You need to look into before and after circumstances that the individual has experienced to establish any relevant context to analyze the incident.

"I was a victim of an stomach stapling issue in 1980 and, during the course of treatment, had to undergo surgery to have a deformed spleen removed. I suffered hemorrhage while on the operating table and the doctor told me that at least three times that he would lose me. The day following surgery, I was required to receive transfusions. One of the transfusions, I started feeling very strange. I was feeling like if I closed my eyes, I'd never again open them. I made a call to the nurse. She said it was all in my head and then left the room. I recall her walking out the door , and I began to be pulled through the tunnel. It was an awful experience as everything I was able to see was people from my previous life, people who were already dead, and were involved in or had said something that caused me harm in one way or the other. They were screaming and laughing until I couldn't take it anymore. I begged and pleaded that I could return. I could see a light at other end, but I never came near it. In a flash, I found myself back in bed, thankful that I didn't die."

Richards As it is revealed, has experienced numerous near-death experiences over the course of his life.

"My mother once told me that when she discovered she was expecting me, she was praying that I would not die. They were only getting over the depression and had a baby but couldn't afford another. The day I came into the world I was born with an hairy harelip. Mother believed that it was punishment for her having me dead. After a few days, and with no operation, my harelip has healed, and I do not have an injury. I was also told that at two weeks old, she walked into my bassinet and discovered that I was not breathing. My eyes had already turned purple. She took me by the hand, shook me, then blew into my face till I began breathing again. I'm not sure if I remember this incident however I do remember that I was in a bassinet which was without a liner. I recall studying my hands and how my hands appeared like when I was a baby. My mother claimed that I could not possibly be able to remember this however I did and I was correct."

From the age of 4, Richards survived numerous nearly fatal accidents that resulted in the loss of breath. The memories she has of them are precise and confirmed by her relatives even though many were only just a toddler. From the beginning of her life (I believe it was when she was only barely a few weeks old) she showed the usual after-effects of the near-death experience that included astonishingly precise psychic abilities, a wide perception, and increased abilities. He has been visited by dead, "advised" of pending deaths, and knows when people passed away.

But Richards was haunted all her life, not only by the dead who held her close in the tunnel of death. A recurring theme "Why should anyone ever would want to hurt me?" appears to have permeated all of her experiences, from her memories of terrifying creatures crawling into her bedroom when she was a child and causing her to cry and cry to adult miscommunications and disturbing nightmares. It's as if her mother's wish that she died had engraved her brain in some way. I'm saying this because Richards numerous encounters with death, when she was a child were triggered by self-destructive behaviors. This single overshadowing motif kept bringing down the joy that her numerous achievements in life ought to have given her. It was not changed until after her husband's death in 1983. In 1983, according to Richards her son and father who had passed away and her deceased husband physically and with a bright, day-light she drove towards her door in a vintage Cadillac she honked her hornand announced, "We're together now and we're fine. We wanted you to be aware." The group, including the car vanished. The ghostly scene provided Richards the confidence she needed to finally let go of that "ghost" from her personal past. The death order of her mother that she had subliminally attempted to justify and defy through her entire life was removed from her mind following the suicide of her husband, which forced her to face the challenges of her own life in order to come to terms with his death.

In Richards case, the near-death incident was just one of an extensive sequence of similar incidents that eventually brought her to a place of peace within herself , where real forgiveness and understanding reside.

Therapy and getting help following the trauma of a near-death experience

It's not surprising that psychiatrists are fascinated by the topic of NDEs due to our fascination with the brain and the mind. NDEs are believed to be affecting nearly one third of those who have had a contact with death, which is approximately 5 percent from all Americans. The number of people reporting NDEs is higher than the total number of people suffering from bipolar disorder and schizophrenia together, which means it is likely that psychiatrists will meet individuals in the field referred to in the field as "experiencers," or NDE experiencedrs, for short, at certain points in their professional careers.

There are a few NDE participants are forthcoming about their experiences, and numerous have experienced reactions that border on the catastrophic from healthcare professionals relatives, friends and even clergy. A sense of trust must be built before they are able to trust to share details of their experience. Being able to demonstrate that you're an individual who is able to listen with respect is a big help in allowing disclosure.

It is reported across every demographic group possible that NDE experienced people are not significantly different from those who have not experienced it. All ages of people from young to very old have reported NDEs as have males and females, as well as homosexuals and those belonging to the bisexual, gay, lesbian and transgender community. The various forms of religious affiliations and absences of it, from agnostics to the atheists, to Buddhists, Christians, Hindus and indigenous religions, Jews, and Muslims are among the many NDE participants. All races and diverse cultures are covered. Near-suiciders who experience an NDE in their final days have a lot in common with near-suicide completers who don't have an NDE in both terms of demographics as well as psychologically. People with disabilities, such as quadriplegia and blindness have reported having an NDE. A fascinating aside is that those who are blind from birth have reported experiences with vision when they had NDEs. In spite of taking into consideration the possibility that NDE people who experienced the experience were aware of the phenomenon known as NDEs or not there is no distinction in frequency.

A person experiencing an NDE as a whole cannot be considered an indication of psychopathology. It has been demonstrated that those who have experienced NDEs have a similar psychological profile to those who were close to death but didn't experience an NDE. It is interesting to note that of the patients with psychiatric disorders and an NDE There was a tendency towards mentally suffering NDE experiencing people having less complex NDEs.

Numerous associations with psychological states have been studied. NDEs are distinctively different from personal experiences from depersonalization, with NDEs being distinguished by their awe-inspiring nature and the sense of being more authentic than typical daytime alertness , versus the naive nature of depersonalization. There is evidence that NDE participants did achieve a slightly higher score on a scale for dissociation but it wasn't within the psychopathology spectrum. It is also stated that with retrospective studies it's impossible to know whether the increased dissociation is due to an NDE or predated it. Even when something is as an indicator of psychopathology as auditory hallucinations, those experienced by NDE participants were found to have a largely positive information, with inspiring themes that enriched their lives, not creating problems. Other characteristics that are not pathological include fantasy-proneness as well as emotional apathy, but they are not enough to explain the phenomenon.

Most NDE people who experience NDEs are brought to psychiatric care because of concomitant mental illness. The new beliefs they have acquired may be difficult to distinguish from the hyper-religiosity of the condition of manic. Sometimes, reverting back to basic principles and helping the patient identify the symptoms of manic mania (and related dysfunction) will increase the patient's awareness and ability to recognize these signs at a later time. The patient will be able to determine if his or her spiritual fervor or elation appears to be an actual transcendent experience, or if the patient is showing signs of pathology, indicating that a mental illness is underlying and is out of control.

To the eyes of a psychiatrist, many of the symptoms reported by NDEs could be reminiscent of mania. On however, others indicate a shift in grounding that is reminiscent of stages of integrity and generativity. In general, research on NDEs reveal them to be an energizing force to change, usually in the direction of the development of a person and improved well-being. Noyes was the first to conduct a systematic study of the effects after a NDE in the year 1980. About two-thirds of NDE participants reported a different outlook on death or life, with an invulnerability feeling or specialness, as well as a diminished fear of dying. This is in absence of other signs of mania, like speedy speech or the idea of flying, but. NDE people who have experienced NDE report increased appreciation and love for people around them and aregenerally more accepting and compassionate. Friends and family members have confirmed the positive results of NDEs.

Another way that psychiatrists help with NDEs is by taking care of people who are close to the heart of the NDE sufferer and might experience anything from anger or confused to demeaning and be hurt. The same way that a psychiatrist needs to show respect for the NDE sufferer and help them in keeping their function at a high level during the life-altering event the same way, certain family members be supported in doing the same for their own loved relatives.

How can psychiatrists come up with an effective therapeutic stance on an experience that might be unfamiliar to us and over which we be prone to our own doubt or skepticism? I'd like to suggest that an analogy can be drawn from our work with patients suffering from "functional" ailments. We know that a specific proportion of people who are functional are eventually diagnosed with a conventional medical condition that didn't be diagnosed when the symptoms first began and it is therefore important to remain in a state of humour about the illness the patient really suffers from. We assist the patient who is functional to establish a perspective towards the symptoms that is supportive and allows for the most efficient possibility of adjusting when the medical field "catches with the times" with more comprehensive explanations. The recent discussion on the functional patient has us reminded to "attend more closely to the personality that our patients." Also do we need to get to understand the person who suffered from the NDE finding the answers to questions like how the patient views the event and how it has affected the patient as well as his or her family members and how they continues to "live on this planet" as a person who has been altered by something that's not understood within our medical system. It is possible to be of assistance even if the reason is still a mystery to us.

Physics and Meta Physics and Metaphysics
Let's look at the spiritual aspect of this issue for a second. The beliefs of religion regarding life after death, as well as remarks that a certain type of survival has been recognized in Christianity.
The scientifically-based evidence does not necessarily prove anything, but it is a fact. We should also not overlook the fact that the doctrine of bodily resurrection could be more symbolic of Christian theology than the doctrine of immortality of the soul, whichever religious people have thought of.
Examining the different philosophical perspectives regarding survival, one realizes 3 options:
1. A doctrine of "resurrection" in the form of the body is that we are the same as our bodies, and end up being dead until God

"wakes the dead" again and provides us with a brand new body.

2. The theory that" the "immortal soul" We have an immortal soul that survives even after death in a different world. This is referred to as "dualism". The connection between the body and soul is a mystery.

3. The theory is that of "shadow-man" We have other bodies above the physical body (astral and mental etc.) In which we live in other universes.

The third possibility is seldom talked about, is very like the experiences of patients who have shared concerning what they have experienced during their NDE experiences. It is also a part of theosophical doctrines.

Before the advent of science, all religions and cultures acknowledged the existence of universes far beyond the visible world. Heaven and Hell weren't just the residences of the dead they also formed an integral connection with the earthly realm. Each now and then the higher realms became part of everyday life which was regarded as sacred. The prescientific man understood the earth as a part of the universe of a omnipresent God. The reality of the day had infinite depth

As science entered stage, the metaphysical notion of reality was quickly disregarded. In the following years it was just matter that could be studied by scientists. The initial scientific study of nature took place unsupervised however, over the course of time, the idea was proclaimed more insistently that science would eventually give us the "theory of all things". The worldview we have lost in profundity, gained due to its expansiveness and a that was attuned to earth, we were able to discover an infinity of physical space in which each star was revealed to be a type of sun (and it was even more amazing that between these stars, faint areas were discovered to be galaxies that were complete).

Nowadays, we are unable to talk about low and high. The vertical dimension has been removed from our view of the world which is only large and small in physics. This actually means very small and extremely large. Some believe this is too narrow. In the present two counter-cultural movements are in place to revive this view of religion. The end of the 19th century, there was Theosophy which sought to bring back the old worldview through pointing out an existence that was higher dimensions or planes that are intimately linked to our own inner world. They may not be visible to our senses physical but not to the clairvoyant. The clairvoyant can discern and explain these extremely sensual (not the supernatural!) aspects of reality and man. The higher worlds are believed to exist until they vanish into the Light of God. This is a wonderful view, with a lot of slow transitions that are an important element.

The other counter-culture current that has attempted to bring religion and science closer together is more recent The New Age looks for a "holism" (against "atomistic" and "reductionistic" science). The New Age is surprisingly oriented towards quantum physics, specifically quantum Physics, which doesn't speak as much about particles, but rather about the omnipresent Fields. Physics experts like Lazlo discuss what they call the Zero Point Field, which connects everything. This popular perspective has been scathingly criticized by people belonging to the original movement that was mentioned earlier. The whole debate on atomism/holism is an issue of a secondary nature, and is by nature restricted to the visible universe of physics. The debate will never attain the depth is described in the old texts (i.e. our internal consciousness that has numerous layers). If the physical universe is comprised of tiny particles or one Big Field, this knowledge does not shed the light on our personal feelings as well as ideas (except by a symbolic manner) and, of course, consciousness in general. This is, of course, a metaphysical criticismthat does not concern anyone who studies science and puts the entire discussion into an overall context. An attempt to link the human mind (or just to understand it using) Subatomic particles and a quantum field have not impressed me personally. If that's our post-mortem reality, I'd rather be dead as usual! God is not living among photons. He has created a world where photons existas well as other worlds of spirit and soul. The view of materialism, or the idea of God is the only realistic alternative.

Human consciousness transcends that of the body (and the mind) and is part of an unreal world. In line with this New Age track: behind the universe of phenomena is an unifying Field in which everyone is individuals. The more we can connect with this Field and in an NDE experience , this appears to be the case, the greater certainty their perception will gain. The way this happens is also the subject of speculation. What, for instance, do we differentiate within the Field the difference between your and my memory? Also, is it because of some kind of localization? Our DNA (and particularly, the junk-DNA which is the most important segment of our genome, which isn't believed to have any distinct purpose) is responsible for the connection between our brains and the single Field. Could this be proven or in some way?

The attempt to discover the origins of consciousness in the mysterious phenomena of new physics is an extremely futile endeavor as it projects the fullness of reality onto the surface of matter. It doesn't matter which takes place, it doesn't matter what the final result does. It is never able to transcend the narrow nature of physics. Whether it's from the past or modern does not necessarily matter. More important the absolute dualism is constructed between the individual/visible body on one hand, and the invisible Field to the contrary. The finite body is contrasted against the infinite or eternal consciousness. Contrary to this the theosophical perspective is considerably more slow. The transition into the astral realm is thought of as an unimportant event and is followed by a variety of shifts to higher realms. The line between the human and the universal has been drawn to a higher level, making it much easier to talk about the possibility of a person's survival following death. Strange phenomena like out-of-body experiences, communications with dead people, etc are all part of the larger context. The idea of calling consciousness "endless" as well as "omnipresent" is too early of a mystical answer in my opinion, at least to my preferences.

Then, we come to the mind body issue that has been a source of contention. Around 99.99 percent of researchers adhere to an anthropocentric or "naturalistic" conception of consciousness.

Are we all reducible to material or do we have an internal consciousness that cannot be reduced in this way? How do these dimensions interact isn't an answer we can provide (other other than the fact that they do). The issue is that the materialists who deny minds, or dualists who believe in the existence of a mind have found the solution, therefore we should at least recognize the existence of both dimensions. This view is quite similar to the double-aspect theory. It declares that mind and body are two elements of the 3rd (unknown) concept.

What implications do this have on our understanding of the world (where does this internal dimension end up to, if it isn't diminished to the mind?) stays unexplained. It is open to possibilities of subliminal energies and bodies.

Conclusion

The most difficult part of trying to give a story of near-death events is the absence of evidence. Because of their nature, they occur in a way that is hard to document and is difficult to establish. This is, in a way it's almost like a matter of faith.

Although it's not necessary that everyone believe in every detail but being aware of the phenomenon as a whole could be informative and fascinating. Even for those who aren't religious the stories can be fascinating both on a human and medical level. We do know that there is a huge number of people with the same experiences and have been doing it for quite a while.

Instead of debating the truth behind the matter in the realm of near-death experience leaves much for the individual to understand. If you want to know more about the experiences of people who are who are close to death, the vast number of books and the abundance of online resources are available.

This book could serve as a great taster of exploring the possibilities of a world that's beyond our personal. If you are still unsure this book could be an excellent reference on what to expect should you ever find yourself in the middle of death for yourself.

www.ingramcontent.com/pod-product-compliance
Lightning Source LLC
Chambersburg PA
CBHW050407120526
44590CB00015B/1859